Making Music with Mobile Devices

G.W. Childs IV

Course Technology PTR
A part of Cengage Learning

COURSE TECHNOLOGY
CENGAGE Learning™

Australia • Brazil • Japan • Korea • Mexico • Singapore • Spain • United Kingdom • United States

COURSE TECHNOLOGY
CENGAGE Learning

Making Music with Mobile Devices

G.W. Childs IV

Publisher and General Manager,
Course Technology PTR:
Stacy L. Hiquet

Associate Director of Marketing:
Sarah Panella

Manager of Editorial Services:
Heather Talbot

Marketing Manager: Mark Hughes

Acquisitions Editor: Orren Merton

Development Editor:
Cathleen D. Small

Project Editor/Copy Editor:
Cathleen D. Small

Interior Layout Tech: MPS Limited,
A Macmillan Company

Cover Designer: Luke Fletcher

Indexer: Valerie Haynes Perry

Proofreader: Julianna Thibodeaux

For product information and technology assistance, contact us at
Cengage Learning Customer & Sales Support, 1-800-354-9706

For permission to use material from this text or product, submit all requests online at **cengage.com/permissions**

Further permissions questions can be emailed to
permissionrequest@cengage.com

All trademarks are the property of their respective owners.

All images © Cengage Learning unless otherwise noted.

Library of Congress Control Number: 2009942397

ISBN-13: 978-1-4354-5533-7
ISBN-10: 1-4354-5533-9

Course Technology, a part of Cengage Learning
20 Channel Center Street
Boston, MA 02210
USA

Cengage Learning is a leading provider of customized learning solutions with office locations around the globe, including Singapore, the United Kingdom, Australia, Mexico, Brazil, and Japan. Locate your local office at: **international.cengage.com/region**

Cengage Learning products are represented in Canada by Nelson Education, Ltd.

For your lifelong learning solutions, visit **courseptr.com**

Visit our corporate website at **cengage.com**

Printed in the United States of America
1 2 3 4 5 6 7 12 11 10

To my daughter, Taylor:

We've had so much fun with Game Boys and other weird, portable videogames over the years. Thanks for sharing that fun with me, Smokey!

Acknowledgments

My sincerest thanks to all listed. This was a wild time getting this book together. I did a move from one state to another, a major career shift, and more. All of you were with me through the thick of it.

God, I owe everything to you, first and foremost.

My parents: Bill and Suzanne Childs, thanks for believing in me and helping me obtain the knowledge early on that would allow me to do this today.

Amrita Soni: Oh, the amount of stuff you had to hear from me about getting this completed. Thanks for always being there for me. The dinners to help me rest my brain, the movies to help me rest my brain, and the wonderful conversation. Thanks, Foof!

Cathleen Small: We've made it through another. You are like the uber-editor! You always keep this fun and light. And . . . you don't miss anything.

Orren Merton: Thanks for putting up with me and my frantic phone calls. You are a well-oiled machine and a really talented writer. Now that I'm finished, I'm reading your book!

Allison Parchman: For always keeping me in good spirits during the final stretch.

Alex Childs: For also keeping me in good spirits during the final stretch.

Eddie and Judy Briscoe: I truly appreciated your words of encouragement as I began this endeavor. Thanks for always believing in me. I hope you are completely healed by the time you read this, Eddie.

Additional thanks to their family members: Tommy Parchman, Haley Parchman, Lexi Parchman, Jennifer Childs, Will Childs.

Mike Prager: Thanks for getting me involved in this! You're a true friend, and I miss ya.

Christian Petke: Book four, and the album still isn't finished! Either way, thanks for being there for me on those lonely lunch breaks when I'm music-ed out!

Kurt Kurasaki: Always a pleasure. Thanks for being a friend.

Ruby Briscoe: Thanks for the lunches! We had some great conversations.

Ashley Horstman: Thanks for driving me back to Texas when all of this was going on. A truly memorable trip! No more haunted hotels, though . . .

Bret Truchan: Thanks for the help with your excellent software!

Thanks to the 11th St. House: Ramananda Nathanson, Jagadamba Nathanson, Aditi Nathanson, Sruti, Candrabhuti, Kevin Russell. You guys always took my mind off the work with excellent conversation and FOOD!

Mike and Mona Riley: I miss you guys and think about you all the time. You're always in my thoughts and prayers. Thanks for your hospitality and friendship.

Additional thanks to:

Obedia: Fred Maher, Steve Garth, Jayce Murphy, Bob Demaa, Eugene Smith. Ozzie Ozkay Villanova, Mary Catherine Higgins, Jay Tye, Sarah McComas, Chris Jett, Chris Petti, Cindy Wong, createdigitalmusic.com, Jory Prum, Lynda.com, Kirk Werner, Megan A. Read, Mr. and Mrs. David Bush, Mr. and Mrs. John Hoffman, Jon Riley.

About the Author

G.W. Childs IV has written several titles covering all manner of audio excitement, from *Creating Music and Sound for Games* to *Using Reason Onstage: Skill Pack*.

Beginning with a distinguished career in the U.S. Army as an audio and video editor, G.W.'s passion led him to the videogame company owned by George Lucas known as LucasArts, where he worked again as an audio editor, sound designer, and audio engineer on titles such as *The Force Unleashed* and *Star Wars: Knights of the Old Republic II: The Sith Lords*. He was also an actor on *Star Wars: Battlefront*. During this time, G.W. also began freelancing as a sound designer for companies such as Propeller-head, with whom he acted as a sound designer for Reason 3 and Reason 4 factory sound banks, and Cakewalk, where he worked on the sound bank for Rapture.

As a musician, G.W. has played for years in the critically acclaimed musical act Soil & Eclipse (www.soilandeclipse.com) and Deathline International. He has also remixed several well-known acts, such as Ray Charles, James Brown, and Gene Loves Jezebel.

G.W. is also a featured author at Lynda.com. His most recent course is on Reason and Record for live performance. He is also an instructor/technician at Obedia.com.

You can find more information about G.W. at www.gwchilds.com or www.myspace.com/gwchilds4, or you can follow him on Twitter at @gwchilds.

Contents

Chapter 3
Korg DS-10/DS-10 Plus   **40**

Chapter 4
Apple iPhone and iPod Touch   **70**

Chapter 5
BeatMaker   95

Chapter 6
Handheld Studio Integration Part 1   128

Chapter 7
Studio Integration Part 2   146

Appendix: Upcoming Technology   171

Index   174

Introduction

At this moment in time, where you are sitting, there is most likely a cellphone or mobile device of some sort in close proximity. There is an even stronger chance that the mobile device is an iPhone or an iPod or that there is a Game Boy in the house. Whatever the case, you have to admit that in this world, we love our mobile devices.

Regardless of what country you are from, regardless of race or gender, most of us employ at least one form of mobile device for communication, organization, information, and listening to music. But what about making music?

Though the number is still small, with the help of a growing number of programmers and manufacturers, many of us are beginning to employ mobile music-making devices. In the past, we've all been resigned to having to simply wait to make music until we returned to the studio, or we'd carry around a ratty old notebook in which we would jot down our ideas. Additionally, a few brave souls would employ mobile recording devices to simply hum, say, or sing our ideas. (I say "brave" because there is a real fear of these recorded devices full of our raw ideas, as scary as they can be, falling into the wrong hands.) I've even had a few friends who always had a guitar in the trunk of their car, in case they'd be out at the beach and feel a moment of inspiration.

Regardless of your methods in the past, if you've picked up this book, you most likely have a notion that there could be more ways of making music remotely. And since you are holding a book on the subject, you've most likely guessed that you would be right—otherwise, why would this book be here?

This book's purpose is not only to give you new ideas for making music while you are either waiting in the subway or on a break at work, but also to show you how to incorporate those mobile music sessions back into your home studio sessions.

The compositions that I've prized the most in the past have been the ones that I began or was inspired to write in moments of excitement, adventure, and emotion. Don't get me wrong; I have a few that I've enjoyed starting and finishing in the studio as well. However, the songs from outside the studio have something that can't be manufactured by machines or by instruments—they have a story.

Studio songs have memories, too, but when you think back on them, you don't have that grandiose sunset that appears as a memory while you listen to it. You don't have the laughter of kids from the local park; you don't have the warmth of that body next to you that belongs to a special someone who still makes residence in your heart.

The studio is a wonderful place for refining, producing, and completing your music, but when you're in a dark room with no sound and no subjects, it can be hard to find inspiration.

I'll also assume that since you're reading this book, you have a modern musician's penchant for musical gear. And I could also assume that you like mobile devices too, huh? As the author of this book, you can rest assured that I have a love of these devices as well, and through this book, believe me, you will be introduced to a few of them. However, let me emphasize one big fact right here at the beginning: While the device may be small, while the device may be brilliant, while the application that runs on this device may do everything and make beats that would make even the sternest people bob their heads, it will be a wasted purchase if you don't do anything with it.

Sure, you'll be captivated by the lights and sounds and rejoice in how much they helped you pass time through the boredom. But if you don't take the ideas, songs, and sketches that you've made with these devices back into the studio, then they were merely trinkets.

So as you move through this book, definitely pay attention to what's new and what's cool—or if you're reading this book several years later, what *was* cool, what *was* new—but please pay special attention to the sections on incorporating and transferring your mobile compositions onto your studio computer. These steps will let you take those mobile recordings and, through careful editing, refining, and pulling out all of those plug-ins you love so much, make them into that platinum record–worthy song.

By utilizing your mobile devices and finishing your sketches, you'll not only have a catalog of songs with memories and emotion, you'll have made the purchase of your mobile device a worthy investment.

In the first chapter we'll cover basic ideas for incorporating mobile devices into your way of working. I encourage you to read this chapter first before jumping around. When you're finished, feel free to move ahead to devices such as the Game Boy or the iPhone.

Now, I'll step down off of my soapbox and let you move forward to a book that I hope you'll not only enjoy, but that you'll also gain some inspiration from.

Sincerely,

G.W. Childs IV

P.S. Don't forget to check www.gwchilds.com for new reviews, tips, techniques, and videos concerning mobile devices, music software, and video games.

The Benefits of Mobile Music

The day I realized that my practices for working in the studio had changed irrevocably was the day I sat in the coffee shop and recognized that I was hardly ever making music in the studio anymore. Like many people, it all started with a laptop. I bought one because I was on the go a lot, always working somewhere, and I was only getting work done for others and never for myself. I missed the moments of serene bliss that songwriting, beat-making, and all the other beautiful things electronic music provided. I missed being creative!

So, I shelled out some money for a laptop, and all would be corrected. At any moment throughout the day, I could just shut off the world, turn on my laptop, and jam out . . . or so I thought. Here are some examples of where the portability of the laptop did not help at all:

- Waiting for my dinner date to finish up in the restroom. Most people don't bring their laptops with them to restaurants when they're dining with someone else. Additionally, when I've tried, my girlfriend has promptly asked me, "Why are you bringing that with us? Don't you want to spend time with me?"

- Using the restroom. Not to sound crass, but I realized that while enjoying a quiet moment alone in the restroom, rather than reading a magazine, I could be making music. However, bringing a laptop into a restroom is nasty, cumbersome, and also dangerous for the laptop. What if it fell in?

- Waiting on the train, subway, bus, or whichever is applicable for your location. You always see the ads showing people sitting on the station floor having a grand time. But let me point out a few practical flaws. A) How fast can you wrap everything up once the train/bus suddenly appears? B) Have you any idea what occurs on those floors throughout the day? C) There often are many unsavory people moving in and out of these locations who would love to acquire that pretty piece of gear. Do you really want someone knowing you have that $2K or higher laptop on your person and following you out once you reach that dark destination in the middle of the night?

- Driving. When driving, I am completely unable to use my laptop. Not only is it unsafe for other drivers, but it's unsafe for me, and it's completely unproductive.

Don't get me wrong; I'm not saying that having a laptop was a bad idea. I still use it all the time and have completed many a track with it. In fact, I love my laptop! I just wanted a device that would help me capitalize on the creativity that came around when I had no access to any music-making device—like in some of the situations I listed a moment ago.

Thus began my interest in handheld mobile music-making devices, which this book is completely devoted to.

This first chapter simply covers the myriad usages mobile devices can provide. From quick inspiration to quickly capturing inspiration, this chapter gives you some ideas for employing handheld music devices, or HHDs—initials I will use throughout the book when referring to a handheld device.

Types of Devices and Applications Covered in This Book

Before I begin, let me define some of the different portable applications and devices that exist. I will reference the following types of devices and applications throughout the book, so make sure and at least give this section a once-over before going through the rest of the book. Additionally, think of this section as a "What's to come" within this book—a way to familiarize yourself while getting a glimpse at areas that might excite you.

- **Sequencers.** Sequencers let you write an entire song, drum beats, melodies, automation, and so on. Most portable sequencers have their own synthesizer or utilize samples. There are a large number of these for the iPhone, and the Nintendo Game Boy has a small but very popular selection, such as the DS-10 shown in Figure 1.1

Figure 1.1   The DS-10 is one of many sequencer applications designed for portable devices.

and discussed in Chapter 3. You'll hear me use the term "sequence" a lot in this book. When I say this, I mean to program music with a sequencer. The portable versions of these devices are wonderful for those moments when you are waiting on a plane or a bus and you just want to make some music, because they essentially allow you to craft an entire song. You might think that the awkward size of the smaller sequencers could make it more tedious or frustrating. This can be true if you are going for precision. Personally, I've found great inspiration in many of the mistakes, though, which I've built upon later when the portable project was ported to my computer for more intense work and editing. Remember, these are just scratchpads. Later in the book, we'll go over how to take what's on the portable device into your computer for use in programs such as Pro Tools.

- **Multitrack recorders.** Believe it or not, there are several portable multitrack recorders available either as applications or as stand-alone devices. Multitrack recorders allow you to record several tracks together or as overdubs. For example, you could record a guitar track and then for your next track, record a bass line while playing along with the guitar track you recorded previously. These portable multitrack devices and applications are ideal for band practices because they allow you to quickly record raw material with some limited editing capability.

- **Effects.** There are some devices and applications that don't actually make music; they augment or enhance existing sounds and melodies with old favorites such as filters, reverbs, echoes, and so on. While effects are a must for almost every brand of performer, DJs in particular have taken to devices such as the ultra-portable miniKP shown in Figure 1.2. Although you might wonder why something like an effect processor would even be handy in a portable configuration, trust me—there is a method to the madness. The miniKP is battery operated and is essentially pocket-sized, with an XY pad that allows you to easily blend effects. Think about it: You could easily add awesome filter effects to a DJ set after quickly pulling it out of your bag. You could even practice with an iPod on the way into the show. When you couple this device with the KAOSSILATOR, also by Korg, you can perform a whole song and set with effects!

- **Drum machines or beat-makers.** These are basically the same as a sequencer except completely geared toward beatmaking. Portable drum machines and drum machine applications are almost entirely sample based, but they do have some limited sound editing capability. BeatMaker, discussed in Chapter 8, allows some wave editing and can actually record sounds like a sampler (see the upcoming bullet point on samplers) as well as sequence them. See Figure 1.3 for a quick glimpse.

- **Phrase sequencers.** These devices are limited sequencers that usually only allow you to record one to two bars at a time. Once recorded, the melody, beat, and so on will

Figure 1.2   The miniKP is an ultra-portable effects device and filter that can be easily thrown into your bag and taken to any gig. Because it is battery powered, you can even utilize it while sitting on a plane!

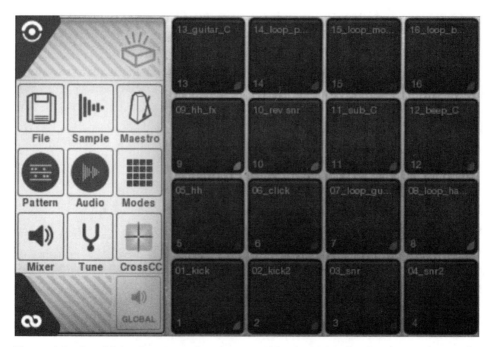

Figure 1.3   BeatMaker is an amazing drum machine/sampler that is advanced enough to sequence your whole song!

loop over and over again. While looping, you have the ability to keep adding more to the loop. Although simple, these devices have become popular for live shows, DJs, and more. The Korg KAOSS line is almost built upon simple and inexpensive devices such as these. But don't let the simplicity and prices fool you; the KAOSSILATOR was one of the most popular music-making devices of 2008 and is still going strong. Of equal interest, you can also find a very similar device inhabiting the Nintendo DS application, Korg DS-10, as well as iPhone applications such as BassLine.

- **Synthesizers.** Believe it or not, there are even portable synthesizer apps and devices that can be quickly thrown in a bag or even in your pocket. On the iPhone, iPod Touch, or Nintendo DS or stand-alone, these devices can be confusing at first because you don't have the usual keyboard to work with. To work around this one shortcoming, many of these devices have XY pads that allow you to move your finger over an X-Y axis. The KAOSS line works entirely on this technology; a great many software applications for portable devices have adopted it as well, such as the Korg DS-10, covered in Chapter 5. There are also many portable MIDI synthesizers that are emerging as laptops become more dominant within the musician arsenal. The Virus Snow, shown in Figure 1.4, is an extremely powerful synthesizer that can be triggered either through a computer or through MIDI, but it easily fits into the front part of your backpack. Even though it's not technically stand-alone, this small device houses some of the most expensive and robust synthesis technology available.

Figure 1.4   The Virus Snow is a tiny synthesizer with a giant sound.

- **Handheld recorders.** Almost every phone on the market can be used as a handheld recorder, and this function has become one that many of us rely on for daily duties such as work, school, and so on. Surprisingly, stand-alone handheld recorders such as the ones made by Olympus, shown in Figure 1.5, are still strong sellers due to their

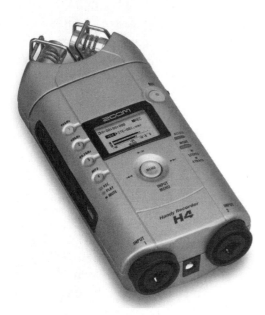

Figure 1.5 Small handheld recorders are very helpful for quickly capturing ideas and sounds.

ease of use and reliability. Even though these devices are simple and the sound quality is somewhat suspect, they are unbelievably handy for quickly recording a hummed melody or a thought. I'll discuss these more in the "Capturing Moments with Handheld Recorders" section later in this chapter. Of additional surprise, I've known more than a few sound designers who have employed these for quick reference recordings. In fact, the concept has become so universal that some of the more popular music manufacturers in the last few years have begun marketing their own recorders. With the musician in mind, these recorders, such as the Zoom H4 (which is also a multitrack recorder) shown in Figure 1.5, are capable of amazing sound quality and even give you the option to use an external mic. Like those mentioned in the earlier multitrack recorder bullet point, these devices are extremely valuable for practice sessions where you need that quick reference recording or just want to capture an amazing session.

- **Reference.** For years we've been using handheld guitar tuners and the like. However, as technology has slowly plodded forward, newer software applications have been showing up on the iPhone, iPod Touch, and other similar devices. Did you know that at this moment in time, you can download a guitar tuner directly to your iPhone from anywhere (see Figure 1.6)? Think about this for a moment. You're at a gig and you look in your bag as you set up for sound check, only to discover that you forgot your guitar tuner! No problem—just download it. Additionally, there are tons of applications out there that give you chord tables and the like. Looking for that chord variation

Figure 1.6   Applications like Guitar Tuner by Alvin Yu are all over for devices such as the iPhone, and they can really save you in a pinch!

of G? An app is out there for you. So, when I refer to reference applications or hardware devices, I'm referring to devices that you can refer to in order to solve a problem.

- **Sampler/sample players.** Samplers are recording devices that allow you to play back recorded audio in either a rhythmic or a melodic fashion. They have been a fundamental and necessary device in all aspects of modern music, from film to most (if not all) current albums. Granted, handheld and portable samplers aren't usually very complex, and they generally lack the overall sound that most sampling software affords. But if you don't mind the grainy, lo-fi recordings (and, as a matter of fact, some people would prefer the lo-fi recordings), these devices are perfect for capturing that quick moment and then turning the audio into something completely different. Turn a car horn into a brass section, turn a garbage lid smash into a snare drum... Samplers allow you to really explore audio, and they exist as either software applications or as hardware. Voice Keyboard for the iPod Touch and iPhone is designed similarly to the classic Casio SK-1 (see Figure 1.7). It allows quick, simple sampling that can also be mapped out to a keyboard that appears onscreen.

- **Experimental.** There are those who would blend visual art with audible art and do so with aplomb. Applications such as Electroplankton for the Nintendo Game Boy DS have been appearing over the last several years and have captured quite a bit of

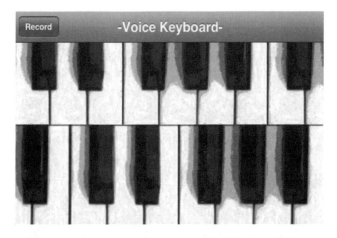

Figure 1.7 Although the Casio SK-1 was a very small keyboard, it's nowhere near as small as an iPhone that actually boasts more ability due to Voice Keyboard!

attention. Being able to evoke music notes from dewdrops rolling off of leaves induces a meditative state, as well as a new way of perceiving music. After all, there is more than just a guitar or a keyboard out there to produce sound. Essentially, experimental devices and applications as referenced within this book are applications that bridge visual art and other senses with sound.

- **Promotional.** What could be a better promotional tool than having your very own software application available for your fans that lets them interact with or listen to your music? Musicians and acts of all levels of notoriety have found wonderful promotion by releasing their own applications for the iPhone and iPod Touch.

- **Controller software and hardware.** Beyond portable devices producing sounds with their own internal instruments, devices such as the iPhone, iPod Touch, and more have the capability to be small and sometimes powerful controllers of other MIDI devices. Imagine moving your fingers across the sleek surface of an iPod Touch and having a synthesizer in the same room reacting to you.

Hopefully, this section whetted your appetite enough to get you excited about moving forward. As you can see, there are many different types of applications, and this book will be a guide through each one. However, don't let the variety intimidate you. These terms, applications, and devices are meant to be tools for inspiration and creativity while you are out and about, while you perform, or even as your main tool for music. What they are not are reasons to stress!

But before going any further, let's talk about portable devices you may already own!

Know Your Existing Technology and Inspiration with Practical Applications

You'd be amazed by how many functions most cell phones come with straight out of the box. The ability to take pictures, remind you of upcoming dates, and record special moments...

Even if you have one of those old, decrepit cell phones that your friends make fun of, you may be surprised to find that deep beneath its antiquity, there lies a device that might spur your creativity.

My mother held on to an old Nokia for years. It caused most of my family to shudder every time it would come into sight. However, I felt a small bit of love for it due to a cool feature that made me (and my mom) smile and beam with pride every time it rang.

Buried deep within the menus of this small phone was a tiny feature that let you program the melody for your own ringtone! Granted, it sounded archaic and akin to something from an old Atari game, but it was true 8-bit music that at the time was coming into vogue for electronic music.

Did I sample the ring and use it later in a track? You bet I did! It was an original melody that I composed on a cell phone, and that is something I always value in a composition— a story behind the composition.

This discovery on my mom's cell phone was definitely a contributing factor to my interest in portable devices. I started examining each menu and submenu carefully on each new phone I purchased. I would even investigate more esoteric technology, such as Palm devices and handheld recorders—especially handheld recorders. Take a look at the next section, where I'll describe a few more features that have been helpful in terms of basic mobile devices.

Capturing the Moment with Handheld Recorders

Let's face it; I've had more songs come about from just driving around in my car than I've ever had simply sitting in front of a keyboard. And this makes sense for a few reasons.

First, I'm relaxed when I'm driving (unless there's traffic, of course). Second, my mind is on something else rather than making music.

I'm sure you've experienced this as well. Think about it: It's a hot summer day, and it's completely gorgeous outside. You're driving along reveling in the beauty of the moment; maybe you're on the way to meet that special someone. As you are moving along, suddenly you discover that you're humming a catchy little melody that just intensifies the smile that's growing on your face.

These are the moments that I've learned to capitalize on! In fact, I've gotten to the point that I don't even turn on the car radio anymore, because the car is that much of a place of inspiration for me!

There's only one problem: The ideas can be forgotten . . . easily.

This is where a mobile recording device can come in really handy, as I'm sure you have guessed. Not only can it help you capture those embarrassing moments of whistling, humming, and bopping and a-groovin, it can also help you capture valuable ideas, thoughts, lyrics, and even sound FX.

Capturing melodies and vocals is particularly advantageous if you don't read music. Many people will attempt to write down lyrics, but there's also a vocal melody that only exists in the moment. And when it comes to melodies, you don't really have much choice—if you can't read music, you can't write it down.

I used to keep my handheld recorder in the armrest of my car so at any moment I could just pull out the recorder and press the Record button. However, since cell phones have become more—how shall I put it?—multifaceted, I have begun to keep my iPhone primed and ready with the Voice Record app already open.

Beyond the car, however, voice recording apps, devices, and so on can also play a huge role in your creative life because, let's face it, there are many moments in a day when you might feel creative.

For example, sitting at your desk at work, where you spend a ton of time, you may tend to have moments of creativity because you're actively working your brain. I've had many moments when melodies would glide through my skull with nowhere to go because I had no way to record the melody!

Again, devices such as the iPhone, the iPhone Touch, the new Motorola phones, and the new Samsung phones all have voice recorders on hand, so know your technology and know the capabilities of what you have on you!

Next, let's talk about another common and overlooked cell phone or portable device feature that is also essential for creativity and project management!

Calendars

Whether you are creating an album for a record label or pushing yourself to get to the point where you have the contract to make an album for a record label, calendars are your friend.

Obviously, this short section is of a more mundane nature, but I felt it did merit some attention, as calendars have saved me several times in the past. The most significant feature of mobile phone calendars is definitely the auto-reminder.

Available on all mobile phones that I've heard of and shown in Figure 1.8, you can set up calendar reminders for various areas of your life. And this is a wonderful thing, especially if you are a musician, an artist, a sound designer, or anyone else who wants to get into the music business. Why? Because that album won't make itself.

Figure 1.8   Believe it or not, mobile phone calendar programs can make a huge difference in completing music projects.

Rely on mobile calendars to remind you of band practices, shows, important engagements, and my favorite: project milestones.

Setting milestones for yourself in any creative endeavor can mean the difference between project completion and project failure. Simply set four or more dates that are actually short-term goals. For example, Monday, June 23, 2012, I pledge to have three songs for my up-and-coming album complete. Program it into your calendar and have the calendar remind you a few days before that date.

Because I'm sure you've gotten the idea about this particular useful mobile device feature, I won't spend much more time on it. However, I implore you to implement auto-reminders in your creative endeavors—they do help you complete projects, and they can be found on every phone and even on iPods.

Mobile Phone Cameras

You might wonder why I would mention mobile phone cameras, but during my work as a sound designer, I've found pictures to be quite handy for sounds that I've created. The main reason is that I can use the pictures to help me re-create the sound if it becomes lost and if I'd like to share the story of the sound's inception later.

Additionally, I've used cell phones to take pictures of sheet music that I can print out later (yes, it was a little hard to read, but you get lucky sometimes), and I've used my cell phone camera to take a picture of my band's set list before the show started, so I'd have a pocket-sized set list during the performance.

What's Current for Handheld Devices

Not long ago, I performed in Washington, DC, where my band shared the stage with another act known as Das Ich. As they were setting up, I noticed that they had a KAOSSILATOR taped to one of their keyboards. (Das Ich is still predominantly an underground act, but they've enjoyed a strong following within their genre of music, goth/industrial—see Figure 1.9.)

Figure 1.9 Das Ich is an emerging act that has known broad popularity within the goth/industrial genre. They employ portable devices on stage.

Acts have been emerging, such as Covox (see Figure 1.10), that not only take advantage of mobile devices like the Game Boy for live performance, they use *only* devices like the Game Boy. Imagine two to four Game Boys working together, and you'll get the idea.

Figure 1.10   Acts such as Covox are known for only using Game Boys in their live performances and recordings.

In fact, over the last several years, a growing movement of not only gamers, but also fans of a more digital sound have taken music literally into their own hands and have taken music in a whole new direction with a genre known as *8-bit*—a genre that Covox finds itself a part of as well.

In recent years, whole albums have been released on Nintendo cartridges—full songs played beautifully and polished, running on the Nintendo's own 8-bit synth engine, as opposed to actual recorded audio.

At first, when you would hear a track off of one of the 8-bit Nintendo-released albums, you would actually think you were only listening to video game music—and to some extent, you'd be right. However, you're actually hearing music lovingly composed on the same instrument all of the classic Nintendo games were composed on—the Nintendo itself. That's why it can be confusing at first, but as you listen more, you'll discover that the same artistry and love that we all embed so deeply in our compositions is there in these digital beats and melodies.

Obviously, if there is music being composed on a Nintendo, then it must have been inspired to some degree by video games. This is true, and it is by all means the creative expression of a new generation of musicians and songwriters who are using something they grew up with on the long road trips to grandmothers' houses and while passing time in between classes—devices such as the Nintendo Game Boy and others like it.

As I've listened to some of these handheld compositions, I've been forced to really re-listen to and appreciate some of the games I grew up with, such as *The Legend of Zelda* and *Tetris* (see Figure 1.11). Often, friends and I wouldn't really regard the music that played in the background of these classic games, but we would still be humming the themes as we went sleep that night.

The familiarity and the nostalgia have indeed helped this smaller genre grow with a hint of the loyalty among gamers. But this growth hasn't gone unnoticed.

Major players, such as Timbaland, have made use of the 8-bit sound as well, though somewhat controversially. Timbaland had in fact experienced some legal issues after mistaking an 8-bit composition owned by record label Kernel Records for video game music.

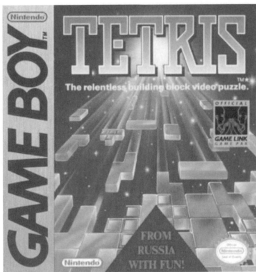

Figure 1.11   *The Legend of Zelda* had a beautiful soundtrack that was both epic and melodic, while *Tetris* had a more mysterious and intricate theme that was actually Russian classical.

Ironically, not long after this incident, Timbaland, in conjunction with Rockstar, released a beautiful application for the PSP known as Beaterator (see Figure 1.12). It utilizes loops, sounds, and percussion designed by Timbaland himself and is, in fact, a very cool music-making tool that I'll cover in a later chapter.

Figure 1.12   Beaterator is a robust music application by Timbaland and Rockstar.

Beaterator itself goes beyond some of the older handheld applications by allowing sampling as well as limited audio editing. This makes it worthy of a look from any musician out there, because it is essentially a studio for your pocket, while at the same time being simple enough for kids.

As you can see, there is some growth and movement with handheld music. Regardless of whether it is your goal to just incorporate a small device while you are on the road for inspiration or to actually perform live with nothing but a device for your pocket, within this book you will find an in-depth look at a large collection of the tools you'll need.

This last section has undoubtedly changed since I've written this, as this world is moving faster and faster every day. That being said, I encourage you to keep up with websites such as www.createdigitalmusic.com, www.8bitcollective.com, and occasionally www.kvraudio.com, as there could be something even better than what's in this book after publication.

Moving Forward

Now that we have some of the basics out of the way, let's move on to the pure task of this book: integrating portable audio into your studios and hopefully into your lifestyle. Because only by adopting something into your lifestyle can you ever truly embrace it and make it a habit.

In the coming chapters, we'll cover powerhouse applications such as the Korg DS-10, as well as some of the brilliant yet more underground Nintendo music applications. Additionally, we'll cover the ever-growing and oh-so-popular iPhone/iPod Touch applications. In the next chapter, get ready to explore the ever-growing world of the Nintendo Game Boy.

2 Nintendo Game Boy

The Nintendo Game Boy line of handheld video game devices is one of the oldest, most famous, and most beloved handheld computers. It has a line of games that go back to its original release in 1989. Besides being a gaming device, the original all the way up to the current Game Boy DSi all sport built-in synthesizers. Although the built-in synthesizer was intended for video game music, due to its quirky and unique "sound," it has been widely sampled, tweaked, and modified by more than a few illustrious programmers and fans of true music production—despite the fact that Nintendo and its developers have mostly left it alone in terms of music production, with some exceptions explored later in this book.

Personally, I've been carrying one or two Game Boys around in my backpack for a few years while I've been touring and traveling. As I mentioned in Chapter 1, in some cases it has just been easier and more fun to compose a little music on a Game Boy than to pull out the laptop. And although my usual software isn't available on the Game Boy, this hasn't necessarily been a bad thing.

For one thing, the Game Boy and its interface, consisting of only a few buttons (as opposed to a whole keyboard), make you approach music-making differently, causing you to think outside of your usual box. Additionally, with its unique, lo-fi sound and a sound palette that isn't necessarily readily available to many of the sound libraries that ship with most music-making applications, I've been able to introduce some really cool sounds to my mixes that leave people asking, "Where did that sound come from?"

In this chapter, we're going to discuss, as you may have already guessed, the Game Boy as a music platform. We'll go over some of the applications that are out there for sale as well as for download and some things to consider for and against using this device within your productions.

But first, let's talk about some of the different Game Boy models.

The Game Boy Family

As you know, the Game Boy has been around for quite some time, and Nintendo has been refining it, as they should, as the years have passed. In this section, let's talk about some of the most popular Game Boys that are being used for music production.

■ **The original Game Boy.** For many of the 8-bit artists out there, the original Game Boy (see Figure 2.1) is the Stradivarius, the American Fender—a beloved tool that is preferred over the newer models. The built-in synthesizer on this Game Boy has a very unique sound that has kept it in regular use, thanks to programs such as Nanoloop that are still running and being supported. However, the cartridges for the Game Boy changed in later models after the Game Boy Advance came around (also shown in Figure 2.1).

Figure 2.1 The original Game Boy is still a major player in the 8-bit Game Boy music scene, although the cartridges changed with the Game Boy Advance.

■ **Nintendo DS.** The Nintendo DS was the first Game Boy to become tactile, meaning it came with a stylus that allowed you to interact with buttons, knobs, and such on the secondary screen at the base of the device. This secondary screen is also the reason for the name: Nintendo DS = Nintendo Dual Screen. In its first incarnation (shown in Figure 2.2), it was almost as bulky as the original Game Boy. However, it has been stripped down significantly since its original release with the Nintendo DS Lite, shown in Figure 2.3. These versions of the Game Boy are capable of using the Game Boy Advance cartridge as well as a port for the main Nintendo DS media (see Figure 2.4).

Figure 2.2   The Nintendo DS was a very big change for the Game Boy series—it added a second processor and a second screen.

Figure 2.3   The Nintendo DS Lite considerably scaled back the bulky frame of the Nintendo DS, making it more portable and more colorful.

■ **Nintendo DSi.** As of this moment, the Nintendo DSi (shown in Figure 2.5) is the latest, greatest, and baddest Game Boy out there. Because it supports a much faster processor than the original DS, it is capable of much more musical potential. For example, the makers of the Korg DS-10 are releasing an update to the much-acclaimed software, optimizing it for the newer processing capabilities of the DSi.

Figure 2.4   The Nintendo DS is capable of using both Game Boy Advance cartridges and native Nintendo DS media, which resembles a small chip.

Figure 2.5   The Nintendo DSi is the newest Game Boy on the block, with more processing power, a camera, a bigger screen, and more.

The new update allows up to four synthesizers where there were only two before, and it now allows up to eight drum tracks. Great news! Beyond additional power, the DSi supports cool functions such as a built-in camera, an SD card slot, a bigger screen, AAC music file capabilities, and more. For more information, check out www.nintendo.com.

Music Applications

Of course the hardware is a blast to look at, but without the software, it's just another game machine. In this section, we'll take a look at some of the music software out there for the Nintendo DS and Game Boy. There might be more than you think; however, there is one thing you should know: Not all of these applications are available for sale. But this is a good thing, because the applications are actually freeware for download. However, I should point out that if you find one you like, look for one of those little PayPal donation buttons to support someone with a good idea.

Since these applications are freeware for download, how do you get them onto your Nintendo DS?

Downloading Game Boy and Nintendo DS Apps

The R4-SDHC, shown in Figure 2.6, is one of the many adapter systems that allows you to transport data from your computer to your Nintendo DS, DSi, and so on.

Figure 2.6   The R4-SDHC allows you to transfer Nintendo software from your computer to the Nintendo DS and so on.

The way this device works is quite simple. What is included is a Nintendo DS chip that has a slot to put a Micro SD chip inside of it, shown here in Figure 2.7.

There is also a USB adapter with a slot on the end of it for a Micro SD chip, shown in Figure 2.8.

Now, let me explain how this package works. You place a Micro SD chip (shown in Figure 2.9) into the USB adapter and insert this in your computer's USB port.

Figure 2.7   The Nintendo-style chip included in the R4-SDHC package has a small slot for a Micro SD chip inside of it.

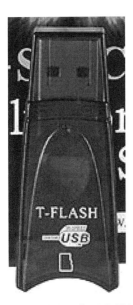

Figure 2.8   The R4-SDHC also includes a USB adapter with a slot for a Micro SD card.

You will need to buy the Micro SD chip. They come in several sizes from a few different manufacturers.

Once the USB device loaded with the chip is in your USB drive, the device should appear as an available storage device on your computer. Simply open up the storage device to

Figure 2.9   Place a Micro SD chip into the USB adapter.

load your empty Micro SD. This can be done the same way you copy any file to any drive. In this case, however, we'll copy repeaterDS onto the Micro SD chip.

1.   Download repeaterDS from www.glitchds.com/download/repeaterds. See Figure 2.10.

Figure 2.10   Download the program first.

2.   A .zip file will download. When it's safely on your machine, open it and copy the repeaterDS folder to the root of your Micro SD card by opening the card and dragging the folder to the blank space of your storage device. Note: This is the same procedure on either PC or Mac. See Figure 2.11.

3.   Now, carefully eject the USB adapter from your computer, making sure to actually click the Eject button if you are on a Mac, as shown in Figure 2.12. This may seem silly, but I've seen many people lose data or cause data corruption by passing on this step. PC users can simply pull the USB adapter out without informing the computer.

4.   Carefully remove the Micro SD card from the USB adapter and place it into the Nintendo-style adapter chip. See Figure 2.13.

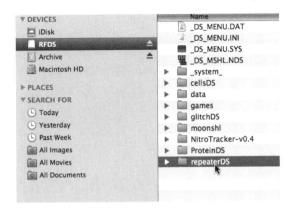

Figure 2.11   Copy the repeaterDS folder to the Micro SD card.

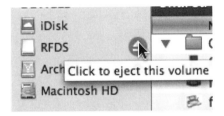

Figure 2.12   When the file is copied over, remove the USB adapter holding the Micro SD card. If you are on a Mac, make sure you click the Eject button.

5. Turn on the Nintendo now. The R4 series of adapters will have their own software that you have to load onto the chip with a special CD that comes with them. This allows you to choose what software you'd like to run from your Micro SD upon startup. Simply choose Repeater.nds, and you've launched your first application.

Keep in mind that there are other adapters out there, but the R4 series tends to get recommended the most in terms of compatibility. Remember, too, that there are several adapters out there, and some of them work for the DS whereas others work for other models of Game Boys. Be sure to check these things out thoroughly before purchasing. Downloadable applications generally have forums that are dedicated to the developers' software. Feel free to go on and ask questions.

One thing that Nintendo has implemented that may completely dissolve the whole arduous process just discussed is the Nintendo DSi's ability to access and download Nintendo's own app store, the Nintendo DSi Shop. Applications such as Electroplankton are now available for purchase instantly and simply require a Wi-Fi connection and a credit card.

Figure 2.13   Remove the Micro SD from the USB adapter and place it into the Nintendo DS–style cartridge adapter.

Now that you have an idea of how to transfer applications to your Nintendo handheld device, let's go over some of the wonderful applications out there. I've taken the liberty of grouping freeware (downloadable) applications in one section and commercial (available for purchase) applications in another.

Freeware Music Applications for the Nintendo DS

Keep in mind that this list may be completely obsolete by the time you read this, as many applications come out regularly. Furthermore, because some of these applications are free, developers can at any moment pull the plug on the availability of said application. Additionally, this is not meant to be *the* comprehensive list of freeware music applications for the DS, but more of an idea of what is out there.

I encourage you to take a good, hard look at the freeware applications that are out there with the commercial releases, even aside from the monetary incentive for doing so. All of the freeware applications are created by regular people like you and me who simply have a passion for music along with new ideas for ways of doing things.

Remember, these applications and more can be found either by simply following a link or by doing a web search. These are a few of the applications that I've found and enjoyed. Imagine what you could find on your own!

repeaterDS

Because we used repeaterDS (www.glitchds.com/about/repeaterds) as our example application for installation, it seems fitting to talk about it first. repeaterDS, shown in Figure 2.14, is a very simple sample playback application... with a twist. You use the touch screen on a Nintendo DS to control the loop points, sample start points, and more. It's completely made for stuttering. But don't let its simplicity throw you off. The motion control of the Nintendo DS is very accurate and expressive, much like a KAOSS pad. With a beat and a couple of samples to work with, you can make a pretty amazing performance out of simple sample playback. In fact, what was a recording of a simple synth tone can instantly become rhythmic or turn into something altogether new.

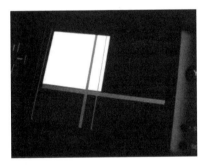

Figure 2.14   repeaterDS is a sample mangling oddity with an extremely expressive GUI.

Thankfully, like many of the freeware music apps out there, repeaterDS allows you to load up your own audio samples. Additionally, it has an amazing ability to lock tempo over Wi-Fi for synchronization with other applications.

Bret Truchan, the developer behind repeaterDS, has developed a small handful of applications for the DS, usually out of afternoon boredom. Inspired by many of the software devices from Native Instruments' Reaktor, Bret sought to make devices that would work on the Nintendo with small personal touches of his own. Can you believe someone just started reading about PAlib (the C library for the DS) and suddenly turned out some custom apps over a few weekends?

Next, let's talk about cellsDS, one of Bret's other weekend creations.

Cells DS

cellsDS (www.glitchds.com/about/cellsds) gives you grid-based step sequencing similar to what is supplied by hardware devices like the Monome and the infamous Tenori-On from Yamaha, both shown in Figure 2.15.

 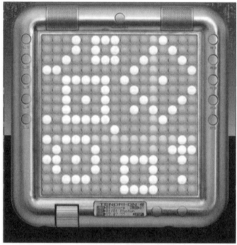

Figure 2.15   The Monome and the Tenori-On are two amazing tools for sequencing and recording. However, they can be quite difficult to obtain.

Two things that both of these instruments have in common are that they are both grid-based and very difficult to obtain. This is where Bret has come through for us again. He's made a free Nintendo DS application capable of doing a lot of what both instruments do.

cellsDS allows you to sequence up to six parts in the same time and gives you the ability to upload your own samples. Through the Lua coding language (if you are a programmer), you can also create your own unique sequencer rules.

As a musician (not a programmer), I found this application to be amazingly inspiring. cellsDS, shown in Figure 2.16, comes with a complete set of unique sounds that you can, of course, replace with your own. However, the ones contained within the application have a really nice, gritty, lo-fi personality.

It doesn't really have a song mode where you can chain together several sequences, but it does allow you to save snapshots of loops you are working on.

With this in mind, it would be difficult to do a complete song with cellsDS; however, for simply making raw loops and performing freestyle with another couple of Nintendo DSes, you could have a very cool live session—especially since it has the Wi-Fi sync mode that all of Bret's applications have.

And let me reiterate that it's free!

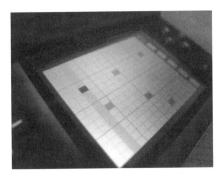

Figure 2.16   cellsDS is a free sequencer with built-in sounds for the Nintendo DS.

Finally, it does have several other Lua sequencer rules available that simply let you use the grid sequencing differently. It's great for live performance or simply new inspiration. For more information, check the link referenced at the beginning of this section, along with cellsDSes free documentation.

Protein[DS]

Protein[DS] (gorgull.googlepages.com/home2), shown in Figure 2.17, is an amazing audio manipulation application that lets you mangle audio along the same lines as repeaterDS. However, Protein[DS] actually shows the waveform and lets you record within the application. It's tons of fun, especially if you are performing along with another handheld device. Even if you aren't, though, Protein[DS] will let you run multiple audio loops at once.

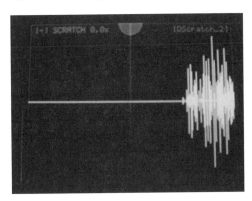

Figure 2.17   Protein[DS] is an amazing audio loop application with the ability to record in real time.

In addition to looping and recording, Protein[DS] also has some light bit-crushing effects for adding a little lo-fi dirt into the mix. But perhaps the most exciting feature of Protein[DS] is the ability to real-time scratch the recording like a DJ—without it costing you a dime.

You'll also want to check out the YouTube videos on the Protein[DS] website. They provide valuable insight into the workings of the application.

NitroTracker

One of the oldest and coolest of the freeware Nintendo DS applications for music, NitroTracker (nitrotracker.tobw.net) is so polished, one can scarcely believe it's free. Shown in Figure 2.18, NitroTracker allows you not only to record audio for use in its highly editable sampler, but also to completely create an entire song using multiple instruments created from your own audio files.

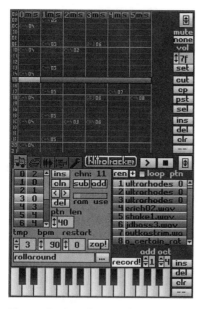

Figure 2.18   NitroTracker is such an amazing application that one can scarcely believe it's free.

As a sequencer, NitroTracker is true to its name and uses an older style of step sequencing in the form of a tracker, which simply lists each note along with basic parameters, such as volume settings, pan, and so on. Although they may look cryptic and somewhat strange at first, trackers allow you to get highly intricate with your compositions without requiring any musical background whatsoever.

If you don't like a particular note that, for example, is the last note you inserted, simply use the directional pad to move back up and press the Del button to delete it. Or if you simply don't like the note, change C-4 to D-4.

A beautiful thing about something like NitroTracker is that it is very easy for someone who has no background in music to begin composing. Additionally, there are some wonderful tutorials out there on YouTube and so on that can get you rolling in no time. NitroTracker does take PayPal donations from the website, so try before you buy; but if you love it, give some back.

Commercial Applications for the Nintendo DS

Now that we've looked at a small portion of the work of some amazingly talented and passionate individuals, let's take a look at what is available for sale. In this book we'll be covering extended usage of a few of these programs, but for now take a moment to get a basic familiarity with them.

Electroplankton by Nintendo

In 2006 (2005 in Japan), Nintendo appeared to start taking notice of the fact that there were some people using Game Boys for more than just games. In a very small effort to encourage this continued practice with their hardware, Nintendo released Electroplankton, shown in Figure 2.19.

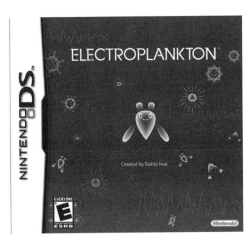

Figure 2.19   Electroplankton is a beautiful multimedia application with a Zen quality not found in many applications out there.

Designed by famed multimedia artist Toshio Iwai, Electroplankton is more than music software and at the same time more than a game. It's art, beautiful art . . . not just in terms of visual art, but in terms of sound as well.

Electroplankton has several different water-based creatures that produce noise by touching, pushing, blowing, and doing all sorts of neat tricks. There are even fish that jump out of water and make sounds when they bounce off certain leaves. Some fish act as samplers as well—you can speak into them, and they repeat your words back to you in strange, affected ways.

Electroplankton is truly beautiful and extremely difficult to find without paying a large amount of money for it. It was a mail-in purchase only, with a limited release. But don't feel bad about this; technically, it's more of a multimedia art program with sounds than a music-making application. It does some cool things, but you will not be able to write a song with it. With that being said, though, it is a wonderful accompaniment for existing songs and live performance.

Here are some uses and benefits of Electroplankton:

- You can use it for random sound generation.

- It's simply amazing running directly into your laptop with real-time effects while recording.

- It's tons of fun and causes you to step outside of your normal work mode and generate melodies you wouldn't normally think of.

Nanoloop

Nanoloop (nanoloop.de) realized that the Game Boy was a viable music platform before Nintendo did. It has been around for years (see Figure 2.20). It originally started out for the regular Game Boy but later added Game Boy Advance support. Currently, it does support the Nintendo DS, but not the touch screen. You have to use buttons and directional pads to navigate, edit, and so on.

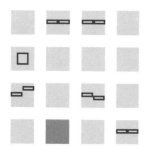

Figure 2.20   Nanoloop is a full-featured step sequencer and synthesizer for the Game Boy Advance and the original Game Boy.

Nanoloop version 1 for the original Game Boy is unique in the sense that it completely utilizes the Nintendo sound chip to generate sound, as opposed to using pre-recorded sounds that are just being triggered. It also lets you actively edit and create custom synthesizer sounds. Version 2 and later for the Game Boy Advance uses a custom software synthesizer with additional editing capability.

There are four Nanoloop tracks available for use that may run simultaneously in version 2.3 and 1.5. Each track is mapped to a synthesizer. Each of the four synthesizers is different and is intended for certain functions—for example, the N track is a noise generator with a filter that one would probably use for drums.

Personally, I've been a huge fan of this application for years. Once you get the hang of it using the well-written user manual, you'll find yourself making some amazingly cool loops and songs before you know it. Additionally, Oliver Wittchow, the program's creator, is highly active in a very enthusiastic group of users. At any point, you can get help from either him or someone else on the dedicated Nanoloop forum at www.nanoloop.com/phpbb2/index.php.

Occasionally, in the past, Oliver has sold MIDI sync adapters from his website that allow you to sync the Game Boy to other MIDI devices. These are highly sought after adapters for studio integration, live performance, and so on. Although there are plenty of plans online for making them yourself, it may not be bad to pick one up when they become available. For more information, please visit the website.

Uses include creating songs, creating loops, and using as a drum machine. Because the sounds are extremely lo-fi, you can get that cool retro electronica sound that has been prevalent in modern hip-hop, electronica, dub-step, house...you name it. I've made several drum patches just by recording individual sounds from Nanoloop. Additionally, you can create some killer dirty old bass lines, lead lines, and more.

Korg DS-10

Korg has been a main contributor to electronic music since their inception. They've released classics such as the MS2000, the M1, the DW-8000, the OASYS, the KAOSSI-LATOR, and more. The list is a mile long.... The main point I make by mentioning them all is that Korg is a major player. So, as you can imagine, it was a surprise when the Korg DS-10, shown in Figure 2.21, was announced for the Nintendo DS.

Figure 2.21 The Korg DS-10 was the first Nintendo DS application to make it easy to get professional results on a handheld device due to a variety of features such as the ability to have multiple Nintendo DSes work together.

In the following chapter, we'll do an in-depth study on the uses of the Korg DS-10, but in the meantime, let me explain that it's the first Nintendo app to make it easy to port your portably engineered music directly into a multitrack scenario. I'll go into full detail when we get to the next chapter!

Connecting Your Game Boy to Your DAW

No matter how cool it is to have a music-making device that fits in your pocket, the Game Boy does not have a keyboard (beyond using a small stylus). Furthermore, it only has a single stereo output. Additionally, there is no MIDI input or output for syncing unless you're an engineer and can make your own adapter. But there are some big reasons to use these small devices, and there are some ways to get those cool lo-fi sounds and beats into your machine in ways that you can get some serious quality and mileage. In this section, we'll talk about connecting your Nintendo DS to a computer. If you are using a regular Game Boy, don't fear—it's the exact same procedure.

Outputs

Despite the fact that the Nintendo DS, Game Boy, and the rest of the family all only have a single stereo 1/8-inch output through adapters, this is hardly a worry. A visit to a local RadioShack or Guitar Center can supply you with the adapters you'll need to connect your Nintendo device directly to your computer, audio interface, or PA system—or however you use it.

Connecting to Your Computer's Built-In Audio Input

If you need to connect only the small 1/8-inch input on your laptop to the audio output of a Game Boy or Nintendo DS, you'll want to invest in a stereo 1/8-inch-to-1/8-inch audio cable. Shown in Figure 2.22, these cables are ultra-cheap, and you probably recognize them from iPod and iPhone usage—for example, connecting an iPod to a car

Figure 2.22   A stereo 1/8-inch plug.

stereo, and so on. You'll want to make sure that it's a stereo cable, especially if you are generating stereo mixes, stereo sound effects, and so on. Otherwise, your recording will not be accurate, and you will miss part of your hard work.

You can tell that a 1/8-inch cable is stereo by the two black bands on the silver connecter shown in Figure 2.22. If it is monophonic, it will have only one black band, as shown in Figure 2.23.

Figure 2.23   A monophonic 1/8-inch plug.

One side of this cable will connect to the Nintendo DS, Game Boy, and so on. The other side will connect to the laptop audio input; see Figure 2.24 for a connection diagram. If you aren't sure which port is the audio input for your laptop, refer to your owner's manual. Most of the time, this port will be labeled with a picture, or it will simply say Input above it.

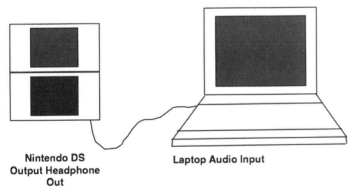

Nintendo DS
Output Headphone
Out

Laptop Audio Input

Figure 2.24   Connect the 1/8-inch cord to your Nintendo DS headphone output and connect the other end to your laptop or desktop audio input.

When the two devices are connected, you'll want to go into your preferred recording application and select the proper input on your laptop. For Pro Tools, this cable will be completely redundant unless you have an adapter, because Pro Tools relies on proprietary audio interfaces to run the actual application. See the next section on connecting to your audio interface.

For example, I'll try connecting to Ableton Live.

1. I launch Ableton Live and go to the Audio page of Preferences. See Figure 2.25.

Figure 2.25   The Audio page of Ableton Preferences.

2. Next, I choose the built-in input of my MacBook Pro for the audio input device, as shown in Figure 2.26.

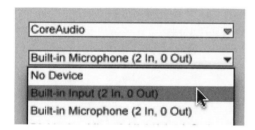

Figure 2.26   Choose the built-in input of the MacBook Pro for the audio input device.

3. After closing the Preferences window, in my desired track's I/O section, I choose the External input and the 1/2 input (which signifies stereo). See Figure 2.27.

4. Now I press the Record Enable button on my audio track, as shown in Figure 2.28.

5. Now I'm ready to record what's coming from my Nintendo DS.

Of course, if you started to record whatever was coming from the Game Boy, Nintendo DS, and so on, you would notice that it was completely out of time with the tempo of Ableton or whatever audio device you are using. And yes, this is a problem for handheld devices, because there are few ways to synchronize the tempos between your DAW (digital audio workstation—the recording application on your computer) and your Game Boy. However, be sure to check out Chapter 6 on advanced studio integration, where I will go over methods for matching tempos and more!

Figure 2.27 Choose these settings for your audio input.

Connecting to Your Audio Interface

If you want to connect your Nintendo DS or other handheld device to your audio interface—for example, an Mbox 2, a MOTU Traveler, or a FireWire 410—you would need a slightly different cable to accurately record what's coming from your handheld device.

The most common connection to all of these devices is the 1/4-inch plug shown in Figure 2.29. It's the usual plug for headphones, guitar amps, and so on. Thankfully, you can find a 1/8-inch-stereo-to-dual-1/4-inch cable easily online and at local music stores.

Figure 2.28   The Ableton Record Enable button.

Figure 2.29   A 1/4-inch plug.

These cables split a stereo 1/8-inch connection to two mono 1/4-inch plugs. Each 1/4-inch connection will go into its own 1/4-inch input on your audio interface, as shown in Figure 2.30.

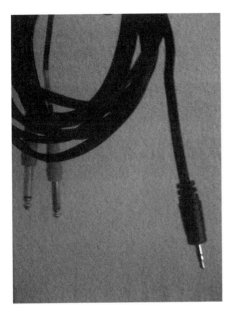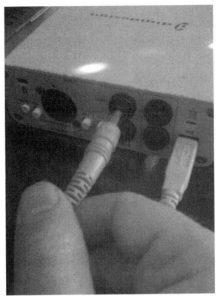

Figure 2.30   A 1/8-inch-to-stereo-1/4-inch cable and a 1/4-inch input on an audio interface.

The reason why each 1/4-inch output gets its own connection on your audio interface is simple: There is one 1/4-inch for the left audio channel and one 1/4-inch for the right audio channel. Remember, even though there's only one output on your handheld device, it's actually sending two channels—one is left, one is right.

Also, while there is such a thing as stereo 1/4-inch, it's not commonly used, and it is never used by pro audio interfaces; they are always mono 1/4-inch connections. Let's try connecting up to an Mbox 2 Mini. Don't worry if you are using a different device or audio recording software other than Pro Tools; it's the same principle with all of them, and we will go deeper into audio connections to your computer in Chapters 6 and 7.

1.   Connect the left channel from the Nintendo DS to the Channel 1 input on the Mbox 2 Mini. (See Figure 2.31.) You may not be able to tell which 1/4-inch connecter from the Nintendo DS is left or right, but you can easily physically reverse this later, or you can just modify the pan settings in Pro Tools. (Hint: Red is usually right.) Also, make sure you press the Mic/DI button for direct input!

2.   Connect the right Nintendo signal to the Channel 2 input on the Mbox Mini (see Figure 2.32).

3.   In Pro Tools, create a stereo audio track and choose 1/2 as the input (see Figure 2.33).

Figure 2.31   Connect the left channel of the Nintendo
DS to the Channel 1 input on the Mbox 2 Mini.

Figure 2.32   Connect the right channel of the Nintendo
DS to the Channel 2 input on the Mbox 2 Mini.

Figure 2.33   Create a stereo audio track in Pro Tools and choose Tracks 1/2 as the input.

4.   Pro Tools will automatically pan Channel 1 to the left and Channel 2 to the right
      so that you hear the Nintendo DS play back the way it's meant to. Now, press the
      Record Arm button and start your Nintendo DS, as shown in Figure 2.34.

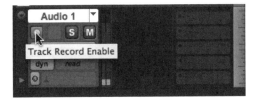

Figure 2.34   Press the Record Arm button and start your Nintendo DS!

Conclusion

In this chapter, you've learned a bit about the Game Boy legacy and some of the exciting applications out there for it. Additionally, you've taken your first steps toward integrating the Game Boy/Nintendo DS with your computer for recording some of the unique sounds and beats that can be generated by the Nintendo devices.

In the next chapter, we'll take a serious, in-depth look into the workings of the Nintendo DS!

3 Korg DS-10/DS-10 Plus

I f someone were to ask me what my favorite portable application is out of all portable applications on all platforms, I would most likely respond with the Korg DS-10, shown in Figure 3.1. This is slightly confusing to me because it's not the best sounding and it's not the best looking . . . but, in my opinion, it is the most fun and versatile.

Figure 3.1   The Korg DS-10 Plus is one of my favorite portable apps out of all the platforms.

Since it was released, my Nintendo DS loaded with the Korg DS-10 has been in my backpack with me wherever I've been. When I'm on tour, I can usually be found making music on my Nintendo (not my laptop) back in the hotel room. When I'm bored, the Nintendo DS with the Korg DS-10 . . . I mean, all the time. It has been a small obsession.

Recently, a newer version of the Korg DS-10 was released, known simply as the Korg DS-10 Plus. This new version, of course, dramatically expands the existing features of the unit, which will be explained later in this chapter.

Anyway, we've established by the drool on the pages that I like it a lot (figuratively speaking—you don't need to wash your hands), but why?

What's the difference between the Korg DS-10 and the Korg DS-10 Plus? Realistically, both versions of the program are almost exactly the same, with the exception of one major difference: If you run the Korg DS-10 Plus on a Nintendo DSi, you get a second set of synthesizers, an extra drum machine, and extra FX. Because the DSi has a faster processor than the Nintendo DS, the DS-10 Plus was optimized for the extra processing capability. You can run the regular DS-10 version on the DSi, and it works fine. You can also run the DS-10 Plus on a regular Nintendo DS; however, you won't get the extra synths, FX, and drum machine. It will behave just like the original Korg DS-10.

What Is the Korg DS-10 Plus?

The Korg DS-10 Plus and the Korg DS-10 original version are small suites of tools consisting of:

■ **2× monophonic synthesizers.** Each synthesizer can be edited, or you can create your own synth patches. There are 4× synthesizers if you are running the Plus version with the Nintendo DSi. See Figure 3.2 for a glimpse of the Synth Edit page.

Figure 3.2   The Synth Edit page of the DS-10 Plus.

■ **1× drum machine.** See Figure 3.3. Each drum part, out of eight parts, has synthesized drums, allowing you to edit existing drums or create your own from scratch. You

actually get two drum machines if you are running the DS-10 Plus version on a
Nintendo DSi, giving you a total of 16 drum parts.

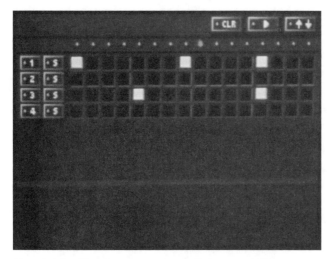

Figure 3.3   The drum sequencer of the DS-10 Plus.

- **1× pattern sequencer with Song mode.** See Figure 3.4. This is actually much cooler
  than it sounds. Each synth actually gets its own pattern-based sequencer that ties into
  the main sequencer. You are allowed to enter notes, velocities, and so on through a
  grid editor, or you can use the mini keyboard to record notes in real time or use the
  KAOSS pad available to each synthesizer as well.

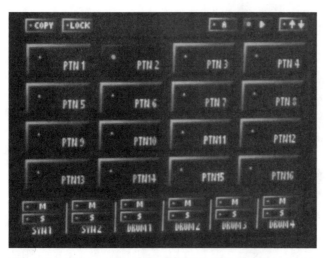

Figure 3.4   The pattern buttons of the DS-10 Plus sequencer.

- **A small bank of FX, including delay, flange, and chorus.** See Figure 3.5. The FX can be routed in different ways, too. For example, you can have delay only on Synth 2, and so on. On the DS-10 Plus, when running a DSi, you actually get two FX banks, as well as FX for drums. We'll talk about the secondary FX bank later.

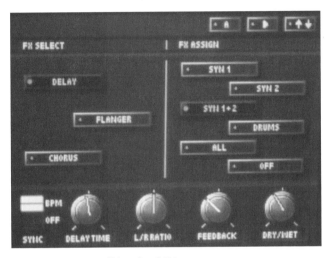

Figure 3.5   A small bank of FX.

- **KAOSS pad features on each synth.** See Figure 3.6. This is a truly stellar feature that sends this application over the top. As mentioned, each synth has a KAOSS pad mode that allows you to use your stylus to draw filter sweeps, gate information, note

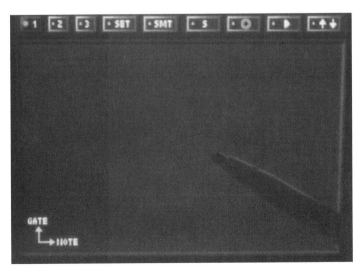

Figure 3.6   The KAOSS pad makes the DS-10 really come to life, making it fun for anyone.

entry like an arpeggiator, and so on. It really makes anyone sound like a pro with very little effort.

- **Ability to network wirelessly multiple Nintendo DSes and DSis (up to four, as long as they all have copies of the Korg DS-10).** This is great for multiple reasons, and we'll explore it more in the FX section of this chapter. But the most obvious reason is that you and your friends can actually work on songs together and be in perfect sync!

If I were to compare the DS-10 Plus to any particular DAW production software out there, the closest would be Propellerhead Reason, shown in Figure 3.7.

Figure 3.7   Reason and the DS-10 Plus are very similar.

Where they are similar is that they do not require any additional hardware—the synths, drums, and FX are all handled by a tiny computer processor. They are both similar as well in the sense that they both pay homage to classical synthesizers, mixers, and so on.

The DS-10 Plus and the older Korg DS-10 version (without the Plus) synthesizers are actually designed after the classic Korg Synthesizer, the MS-10, shown in Figure 3.8—a classic monophonic, dual-oscillator synthesizer with some modular routing using patch cables.

As a matter of fact, the DS-10 includes the same patch area within the Patch Edit screen for modular routing, as well as a very similar knob layout; see Figure 3.9.

Propellerhead actually created another program prior to Reason that directly emulated hardware; it was known as ReBirth and is shown in Figure 3.10.

Figure 3.8 The DS-10 Plus synths are designed after the classic Korg MS-10.

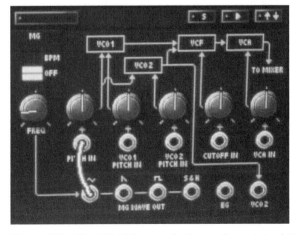

Figure 3.9 The DS-10 is very similar to the original MS-10, especially when you look at the Edit and Patch screens.

Figure 3.10   ReBirth was another creation of Propellerhead that is very similar to the DS-10.

ReBirth was one of the earliest software synth suites and was made up of two software versions of the Roland TB-303 (see the hardware version in Figure 3.11) and two drum machines, directly emulating the Roland TR-808 and the Roland TR-909, shown in Figure 3.12.

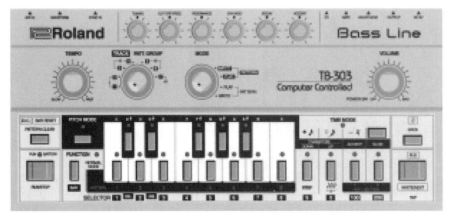

Figure 3.11   The Roland TB-303.

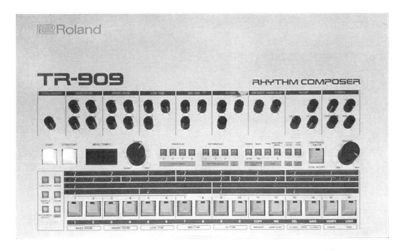

Figure 3.12   The Roland TR-909 and TR-808.

I thought it would be nice to mention ReBirth, as it is free these days, though no longer supported by Propellerhead. Keep in mind that if you're running some of the newer operating systems out there, it may not work. If you have any older systems lying around, they would be very complementary to the DS-10.

Now that we've established a little bit about the history of the DS-10, let's jump into the meat of it and determine why it's a portable application that you should know about!

Getting to Know the Korg DS-10

Getting started with the Korg DS-10 or the newer DS-10 Plus is extremely easy. We'll take a tour together, and I'll walk you through how it works.

You'll start off with the main menu, shown in Figure 3.13.

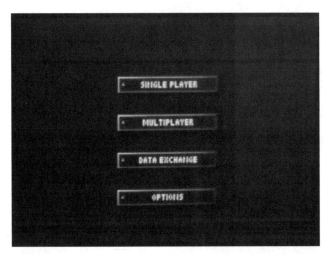

Figure 3.13   The main menu of the Korg DS-10 Plus.

In this menu, you have an option for Single Player, where you work on a standard song. There is also the Multiplayer option, a truly amazing version that lets you wirelessly work with another Nintendo DS running the Korg DS-10 or DS-10 Plus—we'll get into it more later in this chapter.

Then there is the Data Exchange mode, which lets you share songs between different Nintendo DSes wirelessly. For example, if I have a Nintendo DS with the Korg DS-10, and you have a Nintendo DS with the Korg DS-10 Plus, if we are both in the Data Exchange mode, you can download a song that I made and vice versa. Both versions—the DS-10 and the Plus—can read songs from one another, meaning that they are cross-compatible.

Finally, there's the very simple Options portion of the menu that just lets you adjust screen brightness and modify the button configuration.

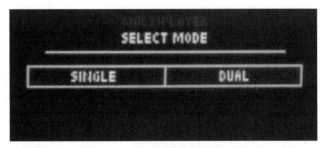

Figure 3.14   If you are using the Plus version of the Korg DS-10 on a Nintendo DSi, you will get this message.

I'll choose Single Player, and because I'm working on a Nintendo DSi, I will be asked whether I want to run in Single mode or Dual mode (see Figure 3.14).

This question will not appear if you're on a Nintendo DS regular or you're running a version of the original Korg DS-10 on a Nintendo DSi.

The Korg DS-10 Plus on a Nintendo DSi, as explained earlier, gives you an extra set of synths and an extra drum machine. It does this by running two versions of the Korg DS-10 side by side that are completely synchronized with one another. Let's see how it works.

I'll choose to go forward in Dual mode, and immediately it will ask me to load a song for Deck A (see Figure 3.15).

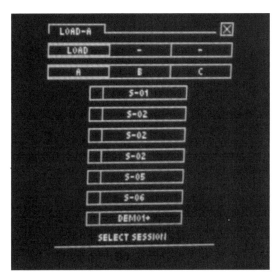

Figure 3.15   In Dual mode, you will load Song A first, for Deck A.

I don't have any at the moment, so I choose S-01, an empty song slot. Next, it will ask me to load a song for Deck B. I choose any old song again, because I don't have any. However, I could press the C button to go to the Song Bank C and choose INIT, for Initialized song—meaning it's empty. This can be handy later on if you are out of song slots, and you just want to start from scratch. See Figure 3.16.

Once my second song is chosen, I finally get inside and play around in the Korg DS-10 Plus for real. And the first screen is more than welcoming, though it may seem a little intimidating at first. You always start with the Syn1 Keyboard down below and the Map screen of the DS-10 Plus above (also the same work area for the DS-10 regular). Figure 3.17 shows a picture of the keyboard I'm referring to.

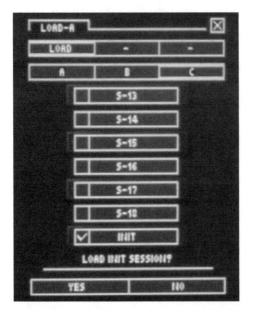

Figure 3.16   Press the C bank to find the INIT song, an empty song with nothing in it.

Figure 3.17   Thankfully, the first screens you see are a keyboard and the Map screen.

Let's break down the Map screen piece by piece, as this is a central portion of the DS-10 that lets you navigate and create—a nexus, if you will. Take a good look at the Map screen on its own in Figure 3.18 and observe the arrows pointing from place to place; it almost explains itself.

As mentioned earlier, when in Dual mode, you basically have two versions of the DS-10 running together at the same time. One iteration of the DS-10 is Deck A; the

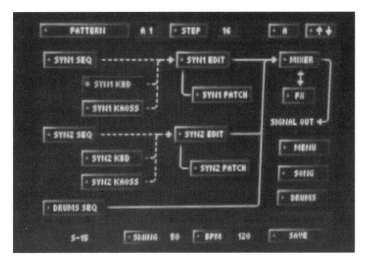

Figure 3.18   The DS-10 Plus Map screen.

other DS-10 iteration is Deck B. While the two decks of DS-10s work together in sync, it's possible to have Deck B synths handling synth melodies and sound FX, while your Deck A is handling the main drums and basses.

Also, although both decks are tied together by the same tempo, they do have some level of independence in terms of mix, groove settings, and more. Remember this explanation of Decks A and B, because they will come up more as this chapter progresses.

The Synthesizers
Look at the Synth 1 section first. It's made up of:

- **Syn1 Seq.** This is the Synthesizer 1 sequencer, where you create notes, edit notes, and so on (see Figure 3.19).

- **Syn1 Kbd.** This button brings up a keyboard where you can play notes on Synthesizer 1. Yes, you can record notes in real time within this application—there's even a Record button and Play button up at the top, found in most screens of the DS-10. See Figure 3.20 and 3.21.

- **Syn1 KAOSS page.** This page, shown in Figure 3.22, may look sparse, but this is where some of the true magic happens. By pressing A on your Nintendo DS or the Play button shown in Figure 3.21, you can hear how much fun it really is. Currently, the bottom-left corner of Figure 3.22 shows that I'm triggering Gate and Note with this KAOSS pad. Essentially, if I drag and hold my stylus to the left, I go down a melodic scale; right will go up the scale. Pushing up with my stylus will cause my

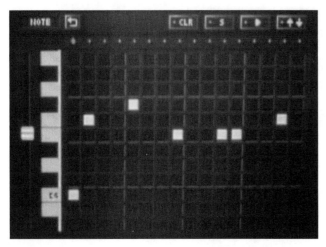

Figure 3.19   The sequencer for Synthesizer 1.

Figure 3.20   The Keyboard page for Synthesizer 1 allows you to manually enter notes in real time using your stylus.

Figure 3.21   There is a Record and a Play button in most pages of the DS-10 Plus.

notes to be either longer in duration or choppier toward the bottom. I can also change the mode of the KAOSS pad by pressing one of the number pads at the top. The 2 button is Volume and Pan; the 3 button is Peak and Cutoff for filter manipulation. All number buttons are shown in the upper-left corner of Figure 3.22.

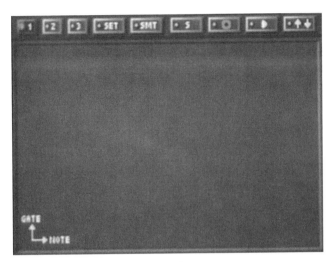

Figure 3.22   The KAOSS page for Syn1.

These three sections in the Map screen, shown more close up in Figure 3.23, are shown pointing into the Syn Edit and Syn Patch buttons.

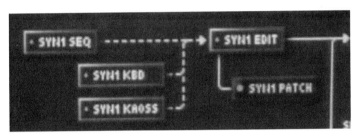

Figure 3.23   Notice how the KBD, KAOSS, and SEQ buttons point to the Syn Edit and Syn Patch buttons.

The Syn Edit section, shown in Figure 3.24, allows you to go in and either create new sounds for Synthesizer 1 or edit existing sounds.

If you would rather work with premade sounds, press the bland rectangular button in the upper-right corner. You will be greeted with a full menu of sounds from which to choose. See Figure 3.25.

You will also notice in Figure 3.25 that there are Save buttons. This means you can save sounds that you've made for use later. The Save As button will also let you save the sound with a custom name of your own; otherwise, the DS-10 will give your patch the name you are saving over.

In the Syn1 Patch page, shown in Figure 3.26, you have a patch bay that lets you route waveforms to parameters such as oscillator pitch, cutoff, and so on. The waveforms are

Figure 3.24   The Syn Edit page allows you to edit the sound for Synthesizer 1.

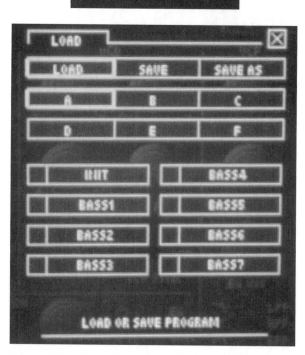

Figure 3.25   Press the rectangular button, and you will be given the option to load preset sounds for Synthesizer 1.

tied to an LFO, with a Freq knob over in the corner. The cool thing is that there are several different waveforms tied to this one Rate knob. You can even route Oscillator 2, or VCO 2, back into itself for some great noise, and more.

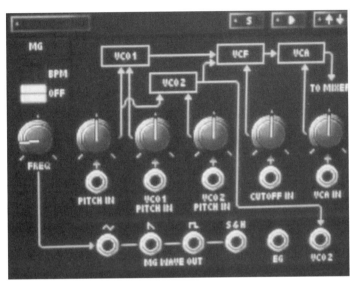

Figure 3.26 The Syn 1 Patch page is a patch bay for routing waveforms to specific parameters for some amazing sound editing for such a small device.

This is all done by dragging virtual cables from one parameter to another, as shown in Figure 3.27.

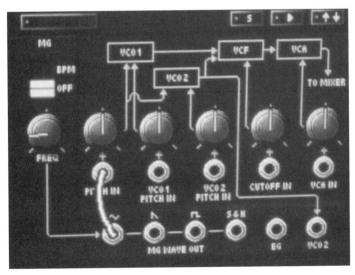

Figure 3.27 You can create unique and brilliant sounds by routing cables from one parameter to another.

I encourage you to try out some of the demo songs, available in the C bank of the song menu, and the preset patches to learn a little more about how to make your own sounds. The best way to learn, though, is just to do it.

The Synthesizer 2 area of the Map screen is identical to Synthesizer 1. It's just a second independent synth with its own sequencer.

A very cool feature of either version of the DS-10 is that you can have a different synthesizer patch per pattern. For example, Synth 1 might be a bass sound in Pattern 1, but in Pattern 5 it's a high-pitched lead sound. Remember to change those sounds around as you progress through your song. This not only helps dynamics, but it gives the track variety. Remember, despite its coolness, the DS-10 has a limited number of instruments, and they can sound tired if they don't change much through the whole track.

The Drum Section

The drums in the DS-10 can be a little confusing at first. But they are surprisingly easy to use and a lot of fun.

For one thing, if you press the Drums button of the Map screen in the lower-right corner (see Figure 3.28), a page with four drum pads will pop up, as shown in Figure 3.29. These pads can be played and recorded in real time by pressing the Record button that is found on most pages.

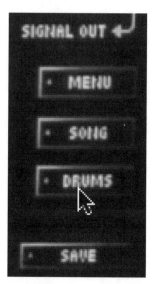

Figure 3.28 Press the Drums button.

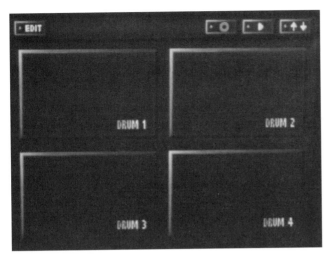

Figure 3.29   The Drums page. Notice the Record button at the top.

What might be a little confusing at first about this very simple page is that by pressing the Edit button in the upper-right corner and then pressing a drum pad, you are actually taken to another synth edit page. This one, however, is dedicated to the drum sound mapped to this particular pad. See Figure 3.30.

Figure 3.30   You can edit and create synthesized drum sounds as well.

You'll also notice the familiar gray box in the upper-left corner, which brings up a menu of preset drum sounds. Again, you can also use this menu to save drum sounds you've made for yourself.

If you need to edit a drum beat you've made, you can go to the Drum Sequencer by pressing the Drum Seq button on the Map screen. In this sequencer area, shown in Figure 3.31, you can edit a drum pattern that you've made or simply draw in drum beats from the get-go with the stylus. By pressing the small number buttons next to the S, or Solo, buttons, you can go deeper into drum programming.

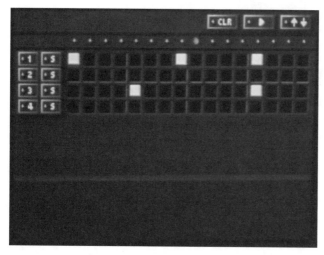

Figure 3.31   The Drum Sequencer.

Pattern Sequencer

Back on the Map screen, if I press the Pattern button in the upper-right corner, a display of several numbered boxes appears (see Figure 3.32). Each box is actually a sequenced pattern consisting of a drum sequencer, a synth sequencer, and synth patch information.

For example, if I just recorded a synth line and a drum beat to go along with it, and then I came over to the Pattern page and pressed one of these boxes, PTN 2, I'd suddenly hear only a kick drum (the default drum sequence) and a beep. If I pressed PTN 1 again, I'd get my recording back.

Songs are created in the DS-10 by creating multiple patterns and then later tying them together in Song mode. More on this later.

It's also possible to copy information from one pattern to another by pressing the Copy button at the top of the page and then tapping the pattern you want to copy information to. Very easy. Again, select a pattern, press the Copy button, and then choose the destination pattern.

You'll notice that there are also Solo and Mute buttons at the bottom, in case you just want to control your whole performance from here. You can solo a kick drum or a synth

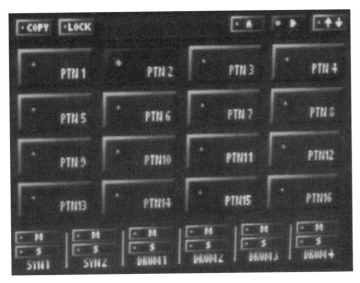

Figure 3.32   The Pattern Sequencer page.

or mute another part. The DS-10 is very versatile and allows for people to use it in many possible ways. These buttons are equally important for tracking to a DAW later, though. If you're planning to isolate the kick drum, Synth 1, Synth 2, snare drum, and so on, you'll need to solo the parts with these buttons or use the Mixer section for tracking, as discussed later in this chapter.

Song Mode

After creating several patterns that make up different parts of your song, you'll want to use Song mode to chain these patterns together. Granted, it's perfectly acceptable to freestyle patterns together, but at some point you might want to actually automate some of your hard work.

The Song Mode button is located in the lower-right corner of the Map screen, as shown in Figure 3.33.

Once you've entered Song mode, you'll notice a large grid with numbers on the left side and numbers at the top. See Figure 3.34.

The numbers on the left side are your pattern numbers. They correspond directly to the patterns in Pattern mode. The numbers at the top are actual measures within your song.

So, if I wanted to have Pattern 1 play for four measures and then have Pattern 2 come in at Measure 5, I would draw four dots up to 4 in the Pattern 1 lane and then draw a dot at Measure 5 under Pattern 2. See Figure 3.35.

Figure 3.33 Press the Song button on the Map screen to go to Song mode.

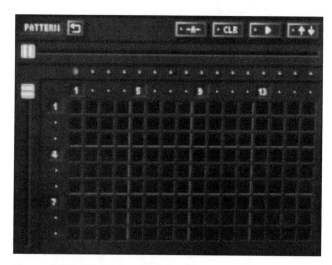

Figure 3.34 The Song mode main page.

When running the DS-10 Plus in Dual mode on a Nintendo DSi within Song mode, you are able to manipulate each deck (see the note on decks earlier in this chapter) in various ways. For example, my Deck B may have patterns made up of sustained notes. One pattern will be a sustained note in the key of C, Pattern 2 will be D#, Pattern 3 might be A, and so on. Deck A would be a more standard pattern of drums with a bass part for Pattern 1, a variation of this for Patterns 3, 4, and so on.

In Song mode, I'll have Pattern 1 on Deck A run for 16 measures, while I'll change patterns multiple times on Deck B, essentially playing different notes as a lead instrument. This is a great way to extend your creative control over the Korg DS-10 and use it as a composition tool.

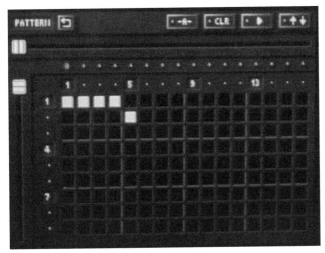

Figure 3.35   Draw in four blocks up to Measure 4 for Pattern 1 and then one block for Pattern 2.

If you press the small round arrow button in the upper-left corner of the Song Mode page (see Figure 3.36), you are taken to Mute mode.

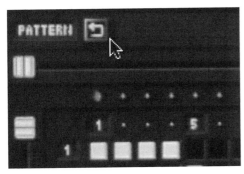

Figure 3.36   This small arrow takes you into Mute mode.

Mute mode is a lot of fun because you can program when certain tracks within a pattern play. For example, Pattern 1 may consist of snare, kick, hi-hat, and Synth 1. Through Mute mode, you can elect to have Synth 1 play for only four measures and then bring in the other parts of the pattern later. Mute mode even has labels along the left side so you know what you are disabling. See Figure 3.37.

It's important to note that Mute mode is only in the DS-10 Plus version. However, it is accessible from either the Nintendo DS or the DSi.

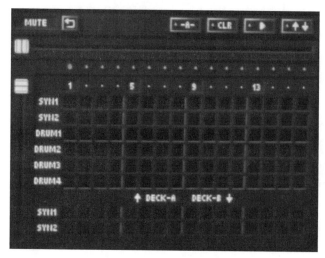

Figure 3.37 Mute mode allows you to selectively play individual tracks in any given pattern, at any given point within your song sequence.

Mixer Section

No studio, be it mobile or stationary, can do without a mixer. The DS-10 is no exception. The DS-10/Plus Mixer section can be accessed by pressing the Mixer button in the upper-right corner of the Map screen. See Figure 3.38.

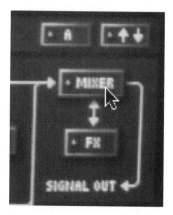

Figure 3.38 Press the Mixer button to access the Mixer page.

Shown in Figure 3.39, the DS-10 Mixer is a very simple version of most modern mixers. Track labels are at the bottom, and there are faders that can be moved up and down with a stylus or a very careful fingernail. Mute and Solo buttons are directly under the Pan knobs, which are the round knobs at the top.

Figure 3.39   The DS-10/Plus Mixer.

If you are unfamiliar with mixers, the faders control the volume of each instrument within your song. The round Pan knobs control which headphone each instrument plays out of. For example, if I turn Synth 1's Pan knob all the way to the left, Synth 1 will only be able to be heard out of the left headphone.

Some people actually prefer to keep the Mixer up when performing a live set because it allows them to fade parts in or out, pan parts, and solo parts as they perform.

The Mixer screen is also extremely handy for recording parts from the DS-10 into your DAW.

FX

Amazingly, and thankfully, the DS-10 and the Plus version both have FX. And, of course, the DS-10 Plus version has two banks of FX in Dual mode on a DSi. Keep in mind that these aren't multimillion-dollar-sounding FX; they are extremely lo-fi, and that's a large part of their charm.

You can access the FX screen from the Map screen by pressing the FX button, as shown in Figure 3.40. Once pressed, you'll see what's also shown in Figure 3.40.

The FX Select area on the left allows you to choose which kind of effect you are going to use: Delay, Chorus, or Flanger. You may only use one effect at a time per deck if you're on the DS-10. However, if you are FX happy, this is another reason to own a DSi with the DS-10 Plus—you get two decks.

Unfortunately, the FX cannot be automated, and they stay the same despite which pattern you are playing on. Therefore, be sure to choose an effect that's complementary and

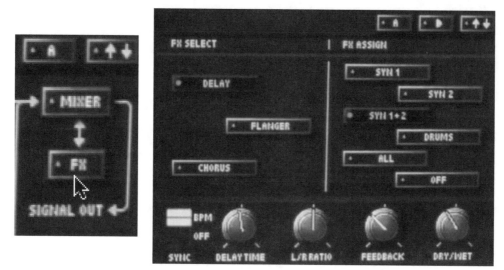

Figure 3.40   Press the FX button to access the FX screen.

bearable through the whole track, or just plan to manually change your FX throughout tracking your recording.

The FX Assign section on the right, shown in Figure 3.41, lets you choose which parts of your song are to have FX. Will it be only Synth 1? Both synths, the drums? All?

Figure 3.41   The FX Assign section.

This is a purely aesthetic choice. Personally, I don't regularly apply FX to my whole mix, but if you're manually changing up FX while you perform, throwing an effect across the whole mix during small segments of the song can have a really cool impact on a performance.

The bottom row of knobs, shown in Figure 3.42, allows you to adjust FX parameters. Each knob changes depending on which FX type you've selected.

Figure 3.42 FX modifier knobs.

The BPM switch is of special significance, because it ties FX such as delay to the tempo of the DS-10. For example, if the tempo changes, the echo rate of the delay will increase and decrease. A synched delay is also great for dance music, in the sense that it adds extra ghost hits that intensify the groove and make it more ethereal. Experiment.

Tempo and Swing

Most of us would prefer to be able to make music in varying tempos, not only 120 BPM. The tempo can be modified by pressing the BPM button of the Map screen (see Figure 3.43).

Figure 3.43 Press the BPM button of the Map screen to adjust the tempo of your DS-10/Plus project.

Unfortunately, you can't do tempo automation, but if you record your final project within Ableton Live, Logic, or Pro Tools, this won't be much of a problem due to their real-time warping abilities.

If the sequencer is a little too perfect in the sense that it feels very robotic, you can add a little swing into your recording by pressing the Swing button within the Map screen. No swing is 50, and it goes all the way to 70. See Figure 3.44.

Basically, swing takes recorded notes in the DS-10 slightly out of time, giving them more of a groovy feel. For hip-hop, house, various forms of techno, and more, having a little swing is a necessity.

Suggestions for Integration

The DS-10/Plus is almost designed as an all-in-one portable studio that doesn't really give any clue as to how you could use it outside of your Nintendo DS. It doesn't in any way tell you how you could have it work with a computer; none of this is there. This

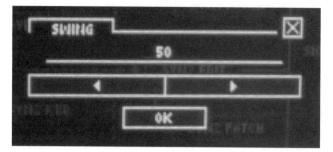

Figure 3.44   The Swing screen.

book does give a lot of suggestions for that, though—some of them are in Chapters 6 and 7, which are dedicated to studio integration. However, I have some special suggestions in this section of this chapter.

Panning

If you are using an audio interface, it is perfectly acceptable to pan Synth 1 to the far left within the Mixer screen and maybe the kick drum to the right. See Figure 3.45.

Figure 3.45   Pan Synth 1 to the left and the kick to the right.

In Pro Tools, when you're recording your work, set up two audio tracks. Set the input of one of your audio tracks to the channel input that has the left channel coming from your Nintendo DS, and then set the input of your other audio track to the right channel coming from your Nintendo DS. See Figure 3.46.

Figure 3.46   Set up your tracks in Pro Tools.

Because Synth 1 is panned to the left and your kick drum is to the right, you now have two dedicated instrument lines coming from your Nintendo DS. Even if you only plan on recording Synth 1, you can still use the kick track as a tempo reference. You don't even have to record the kick; just match it to the click track in Pro Tools.

Using the Multiplayer Mode for Recording

You can expand on the previous suggestion if you have more than one copy of the DS-10, along with more than one Nintendo DS.

For example, if I have three Nintendo DSes, each with a copy of the Korg DS-10, I can use the Data Exchange mode to transfer my song to all three DSes. Next, if I have an audio interface with multiple audio inputs, I can send a right and left signal from each Nintendo DS. See the diagram in Figure 3.47.

Next, I can dedicate:

■   The left channel from Nintendo DS 1 to my kick goes to mono channel 1 in Pro Tools.

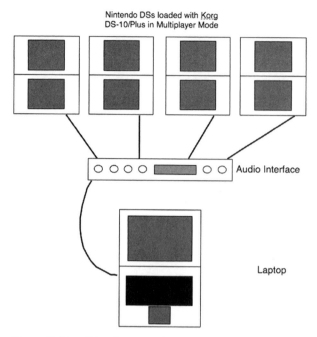

Figure 3.47 This diagram shows the connection of multiple Nintendo DSes to an audio interface.

- The right channel from Nintendo DS 1 as my bass goes to mono channel 2 in Pro Tools.

- The left channel from Nintendo DS 2 is my bell sound and goes to mono channel 3 in Pro Tools.

- The right channel from the Nintendo DS 2 is my hi-hat and goes to mono channel 4 in Pro Tools.

- The left channel from the Nintendo DS 3 is my snare and goes to mono channel 5 in Pro Tools.

- The right channel from the Nintendo DS 3 is my crash and goes to mono channel 6 in Pro Tools.

Now, as long as I record enable each track within Pro Tools, and as long as all of my Nintendo DSes are set up in Multiplayer mode (see the manual), when I press the Record button in Pro Tools, all of my Nintendo DSes will be recorded simultaneously and in perfect sync. If they aren't in sync with Pro Tools—and this is almost assuredly the case, as the DS-10 has no external sync feature—you can refer to Chapter 6 for tempo correction after it's all recorded.

Conclusion

I had such a good time writing this chapter and showing it to you. When I try to en-lighten most people about the DS-10, their eyes tend to get glassy quickly, and they want to change the subject. Later, they'll hear what it can do and ask me how I got that unique lo-fi sound, and I'll try to tell them again. Then their eyes will glaze over again.

Even though it may at times seem complicated, it's really quite simple and a lot of fun. Don't get too caught up in what's supposed to do what; play with it and make it do what you think it should do!

4 Apple iPhone and iPod Touch

I don't think there's ever been a device that has made quite as big of a stir as the iPhone. I was actually there at Macworld when Apple announced this insanely powerful device. I'll never forget the shock and awe I felt as I watched a demonstration of how the device worked. I couldn't help but think to myself, "This is at least seven years ahead of anything that's out there right now."

I mean, when they released the iPhone and then the iPod Touch shortly after, nothing out there had a touch screen as powerful or as tactile as these devices. Nothing out there was as simple and fun to use. But unfortunately, it would take a few more years of updates for the iPhone and Touch to be ready for the third-party-developed applications. Well, at least for legitimate third-party applications...

At the beginning, upon launch, many inspired programmers couldn't wait for Apple to open the door to third-party development. Jailbreaking occurred, where you would run an application that would "jailbreak" your phone and allow you to use third-party applications. However, Apple did not condone this, and you did so at your own peril. Several phones were "bricked," or made completely inoperable due to Apple updates that wrote over "jailbroken" phones, and as you know, these have never been cheap devices.

It wasn't until Apple opened up third-party development with the long-awaited developers kit and the App Store came about that solid and highly usable music applications came around—applications for controlling other applications, applications that make the iPhone/iPod Touch complete musical instruments, applications for musical reference, and more. And to this day, new applications are coming out literally every minute.

In this chapter, we'll go over the iPhone/iPod basics in terms of models, applications, and tips for getting started making music on the iPhone and iPod Touch. Let's get started.

iPhone or iPod Touch: Does It Matter?

Before we move any further, let's take a quick second to go over the differences between the iPhone and iPod Touch and discuss how these differences can affect music applications you might purchase.

The main difference between the two devices is the simple fact that the iPhone always has an Internet connection, unless you have no signal or you are in Airplane Mode, thus disabling all phone capabilities. Beyond this, the iPod Touch and the iPhone can both connect to the Internet, though the iPod Touch can only connect through a Wi-Fi connection (a wireless router), whereas the iPhone connects through the 3G network, the Edge network, or Wi-Fi.

Additionally, the 3GS model of iPhone allows you to record video and offers faster processing all around. Video doesn't necessarily mean a lot for music applications, but it can be handy for band practices and such.

So, what's the bottom line? What advantage does the iPhone really give you over the iPod Touch? There really isn't one. However, you should always check out the product descriptions and requirements before downloading an application—the developer could have a reason for specifying only the iPhone, but personally, I haven't run into a situation like this.

There is one perk with regard to having an iPhone over an iPod Touch. You take an iPod with you most places; you take a phone everywhere. It's a device that everyone relies on. When you make a purchase, you are in a sense committing to using the device. If it's not a device that you'll use all the time, the commitment can die, and the device will just sit in a drawer. If you're serious about handheld music with the iPhone or iPod Touch, make sure you get the device that you know you will have with you all the time. This ensures that you're not only familiar with it, but savvy as well. Especially with those music apps . . .

Applications

Now let's get down to the real reason we're here. In this section I'd like to talk about some of the applications that have really caught my attention as an electronic artist. Remember, there are thousands of applications out there; these are some of the ones I've highlighted for various reasons and that in one way or another can be used for pro audio purposes. Think of this more as my Top 10 list, but keep in mind that if a favorite app of yours is missing, it doesn't mean I'm discounting it as something trivial or unworthy of attention. These are simply applications I've gotten a lot of use out of and would love to tell you about.

Another thing to keep in mind: Out of every handheld device platform out there, Apple's App Store can get new music application arrivals literally at any moment. New applications are constantly being introduced. This is just a small perk!

BeatMaker by Intua

If there had to be one killer music app for the Apple portable family, it would be Beat-Maker (www.intua.net). This application sports almost every feature that the pro applications like Logic Pro and Pro Tools carry, but it fits in your pocket. For starters, it's a pocket sampler with Akai MPC sampler–style pads, shown here in Figure 4.1.

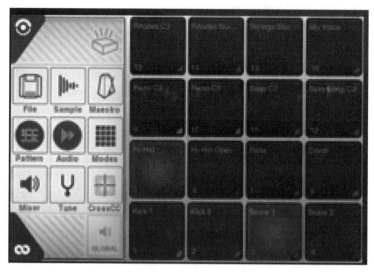

Figure 4.1   BeatMaker actually has Akai MPC–style pads that work!

What's an Akai MPC? The Akai MPC series of samplers are tabletop samplers with built-in sequencers. What makes them special are the multiple large pads that can each be assigned to different loops, sounds, and percussion hits. For hip-hop, house, techno, and so on, these instruments historically have been staple pieces of gear, especially during the '90s, when they were at the heart of many successful artists' studios. See Figure 4.2 for a look!

The pads in BeatMaker, like the original MPC samplers, can be triggered by simply tapping the one that you desire. BeatMaker comes packed with tons of sample kits already filled with loops, percussion, synth sounds, and so on. But it also allows you to record samples directly from the iPhone or iPod Touch.

Beyond recording sounds, you can actually sequence your song entirely in BeatMaker's pattern-based sequencer, shown in Figure 4.3.

Notice its similarity to arrangement sections seen in applications such as Logic Pro, Cubase, and Pro Tools. In fact, it actually works a lot like these applications!

BeatMaker purchasers also have access to another application made by Intua known as BeatPack. This application allows you to share audio from your computer to BeatMaker on your iPhone and to create your own sound packs and so on.

Figure 4.2   Behold, an Akai MPC!

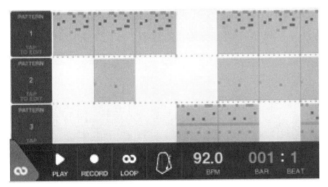

Figure 4.3   BeatMaker has a full-fledged sequencer similar to many pro applications.

When you finish your song in BeatMaker, you can also export it as audio, so that you can pass it along to a friend. Or, you can export the song as MIDI so that you can edit and expand on your portably created track. The MIDI export is a key feature even if you don't tend to finish your handheld songs. You may have just come up with a killer beat that inspires you. This beat can be brought into Logic Pro, for example, and this could lead to a completely new song. You might never have received this beat inspiration simply sitting in front of a computer. Instead, you worked on a song sitting in a park watching beautiful people walk by, sipping a warm coffee. Doesn't that sound more exciting?

If you feel intimidated by all of the features of BeatMaker, don't fret. The next chapter is entirely devoted to it. On to the next app . . .

I Am T-Pain by Smule, Powered by Antares

If you missed "I'm on a Boat," a music video that came out on *Saturday Night Live*—a hilarious skit with music sensation T-Pain—then you'll miss part of the significance of this application. However, you won't miss the significance of a mobile device sporting Antares Auto-Tune functionality.

First, what is Auto-Tune? It was originally designed as a tool for engineers and producers to keep their singers in key. It uses pitch-shifting technology to lightly nudge artists back in pitch and can be set up to keep said vocals within a certain scale and so forth. It's a very cool feature considering you may run into a situation in which a vocal take is awesome, but a few of the notes are quite out of key. Simply add on a little Auto-Tune, and everything is fine—perfect pitch.

Somewhere along the way, like many audio applications, this handy little tool turned into a staple vocal effect that has been present in many, many Top 40 tracks, starting with Cher's "Believe" back in the '90s. In later years Auto-Tune was adopted by the hip-hop and R&B crowd, where it has to this day remained as a main vocal effect for many modern songs.

One artist who has made much use of the Auto-Tune effect is T-Pain. To clue in those of you who don't get the reference, a few years ago on *Saturday Night Live,* the artist guest-starred, and a music video was aired that had T-Pain singing with his signature Auto-Tune effect.

Who would've known it? This small effect and appearance brought obscene amounts of attention to the burgeoning star. But through the viral tendencies of YouTube, this video has endured for years and is still quite popular.

Smule and Antares teamed up to cash in on said success, and in doing so created a novel party app complete with a karaoke machine filled to the brim with T-Pain hits, as well as a real-time vocal effect processor that can be used anywhere. This app is known as I Am T-Pain.

Think about it: You could have essentially a semi-pro version of an effect used by every major artist over the last several years right there on your phone for a small amount of money!

The vocal effect is great, and you can have it keep your voice within a specific scale and so on, but the karaoke machine that comes along with it actually has its uses as well—it's a great scratchpad while on the go.

In addition to having tons of T-Pain songs, there are also basic drum beats that you can sing along to, and I Am T-Pain will record you while you're singing, as shown in Figure 4.4. When you're finished, you can email your work to yourself.

Figure 4.4 I Am T-Pain lets you not only sing along in true karaoke style with T-Pain hits, but also freestyle to beats.

How many times have you been sitting in a hotel room after a tough day and suddenly had the strange realization that you were humming a really cool song you'd just made up? How many times has this happened when you've had nothing to capture the moment? Even if you had a handheld recorder, did you have a drumbeat to sing along to?

Although there is a huge amount of humor surrounding this product, don't discount it. With a simple Composite AV Cable from Apple, shown in Figure 4.5, I was able to use the two audio output cables and some 1/4-inch adapters going from the iPhone to my audio adapter, also shown in Figure 4.5. From here, I was able to sing into Logic Pro in real time, and I actually was able to use the Auto-Tune capabilities with little to no latency. In Chapters 6 and 7, I'll be going into more little tricks like this, where you can integrate the iPhone or iPod Touch into your existing studio rig.

BassLine by Finger-Pro
There are many TB-303 clones out there. You know, the small Roland synthesizer shown in Figure 4.6 that has been emulated by everyone? And while the TB-303 originally was a failure on the market, when it was rediscovered several years after it was released, its unique sound changed dance music forever.

Figure 4.5 Using the Composite AV Cable from Apple, I'm able to use my iPhone as a mic while I Am T-Pain processes my voice in real time.

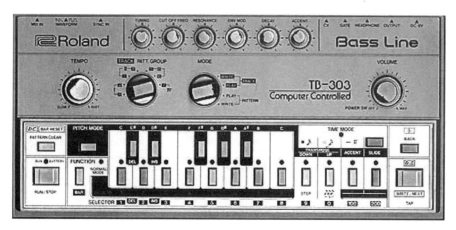

Figure 4.6 The TB-303 was a major failure of a tabletop synth that in the end changed dance music as we know it and is now worth way more than it was when it was released.

Well, of course there would be one or two TB-303 clones in the Apple App Store. And believe me, no one is happier about this than I am. But I've only found one that can actually sync to the MIDI Clock of my host application.

BassLine by Finger-Pro (www.finger-pro.com) comes with a unique application called MidiBroadcast, shown in Figure 4.7 and also made by Finger-Pro, that allows you to sync your BassLine iPhone/iPod Touch app to your DAW's MIDI Clock using the built-in Apple AirPort on all modern Apple computers. What's better is it works! There's no need to tap tempo or align the tempo of the bass line with the drum beat on your

Figure 4.7   MidiBroadcast, available for free from Finger-Pro.com, allows you to sync BassLine to the MIDI Clock of programs such as Logic Pro, Ableton Live, and Pro Tools.

computer. Once MidiBroadcast is set up, it's in perfect time. Just make sure you read the manual to set it up.

But even besides the cool sync feature that MidiBroadcast provides, I couldn't help but be enamored with the sound and usability of BassLine itself, shown in Figure 4.8.

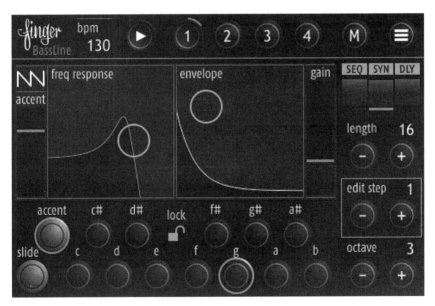

Figure 4.8   BassLine is a simple but beautifully designed app for the iPhone.

Applications such as the DB-303 by Pulse Code, Inc. have opted to go for the nostalgic look of the original TB-303. (See the DB-303 in Figure 4.9.) And believe me, even the audio is quite accurate! However, the BassLine by Finger-Pro is very minimal. There are no knobs to try to turn; it uses only buttons and KAOSS pad–type boxes for adjusting the filter frequency, envelope, and more. I found it very easy to use and very easy to pick up.

There's nothing wrong with the DB-303—far from it—I just prefer the interface of the BassLine as well as its sync feature. I still bought the DB-303, though!

Figure 4.9   The DB-303 by Pulse Code, Inc. is also a wonderful visual and audible re-creation of the original TB-303.

While easy to use, like the TB-303, the DB-303, and every other TB clone out there, the BassLine has a biting and distinctive sound that fits well within any electronic track. And because it's in perfect time when using MidiBroadcast, it's easy to work into a mix. Also, MidiBroadcast came with a very well-written manual; I encourage you to read it if you decide to try this out. Note that MidiBroadcast currently only works with Apple computers. But, don't worry—in Chapter 6, we'll talk about sync tips for mobile devices. MidiBroadcast just makes it much easier.

iTM Apps by iTouchMidi

Of all of the features of the iPod Touch and iPhone, the touch screen is probably one of the most distinctive and memorable. The ability to pinch, drag, and push buttons carries the same amount of coolness that the original mouse did for the early Apple computers when they first came out.

You may not know it, but there is also a MIDI controller out there known as the Lemur, shown in Figure 4.10, that has very similar touch-screen technology. Created by a company called JazzMutant, it's a small computer LCD screen that allows you to move virtual knobs of your own making to control virtual devices in your computer—in fact, even outside of your computer—through the use of MIDI.

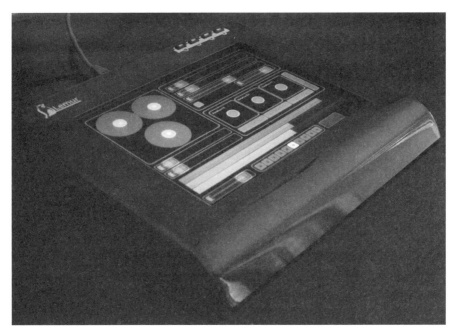

Figure 4.10 The JazzMutant Lemur, a beautiful device that is as colorful as it is useful and elegant.

The Lemur can be purchased through stores for an MSRP of $1,999.99 at the time of this writing. And believe me, it truly is a wonderful piece of kit. But before you run out to buy it, I should mention that you can also emulate some of its features on the iPhone for a slightly lesser amount of money. If you can't handle $1,999.99, do you think you could handle $5.99?

iTM, which stands for iTouchMidi (www.itouchmidi.com), makes a suite of very powerful, tactile MIDI control applications for the iPhone that simply allow you to control parameters of other applications on your computer, be they Mac or PC. It's even GarageBand friendly!

These apps don't make sound themselves; they let you control sound on your computer by simply moving your finger around.

For example, the iTM Keys app, shown in Figure 4.11, is a small application that does what it says: It gives you a musical keyboard on your iPhone that lets you control the instrument on your screen. Maybe the piano in GarageBand? Maybe a bass patch in Logic?

It doesn't work immediately upon download; you'll have to download companion software from www.itouchmidi.com, and yes, you will need to read a manual. But in the end, you'll have a small MIDI controller that cost you $5.99. And, no, you probably won't be able to play "Moonlight Sonata" on it, but it's fine for a quick melody when you don't have a larger MIDI controller.

Figure 4.11 The iTM Keys app lets you use a small keyboard on your iPhone to control the virtual instruments on your computer.

If you're an Ableton fan, there's also the iTM Matrix, shown in Figure 4.12, that lets you trigger clips from Ableton or simply trigger samples. It's a simple grid of buttons that you can assign how you like. Imagine being able to sit in your easy chair banging out beats while your computer is across the room.

Figure 4.12 Play some drum beats or play some Ableton clips with iTM Matrix.

If you're a DJ who uses TRAKTOR or Serato, you may find it enjoyable to move into the crowd while your laptop is still in the background. Don't worry; you can still cue your song when it's time for it to start. The iTM DJ, shown in Figure 4.13, is a simple DJ controller with two faders, cue/play buttons, and even knobs for FX. Keep in mind that

Figure 4.13 DJ your set from around the club with iTM DJ.

it's not a DJ application; it controls other DJ applications. Imagine walking around the club cueing up different tracks! Granted, you won't be able to hear the B-roll.

But while the touch screen thing is cool on the iPhone, remember that the screen is only one controller within the iPhone that can affect an application. Have you seen those games where you can physically tilt the iPhone or iPod Touch to the left, and suddenly the car on the screen starts to veer left?

This technology, which is also inside the iPhone and iPod Touch, is known as the *accelerometer*. It allows programs that are coded to receive signals from the iPod Touch and iPhone to report the X and Y axes of either device.

For example, if I tilt my phone to the side, the accelerometer within the iPhone or iPod Touch reports that the phone has been tilted to the side, thus letting the game know, thus letting the car know to veer to the right.

iTM has capitalized on this technology as well with iTM Tilt, shown in Figure 4.14, which allows you to map functions within your DAW to either the X or Y axis within iTM Tilt and then manipulate these settings by simply moving your phone around with your hand.

Figure 4.14 With iTM Tilt, your phone becomes a magic wand!

For example, within Ableton Live, I mapped the cutoff frequency to the Y axis and the resonance to the X axis. When I tilt my iPhone to the left, this triggers the X axis and causes the resonance to lower. If I tilt my phone forward, this triggers the Y axis and causes the cutoff frequency to raise.

The end result—and believe me, this description is far more sexy than talking about X/Y axes—is that I can glide my iPhone around and affect the sound of a synthesizer live, in real time. Imagine the show possibilities for live performance!

iTM also offers another lovely app that works off the X and Y axes, this time in simple KAOSS pad–styled configurations where you move your hand over a pad. If you move your finger up, you are triggering increments of one parameter mapped, such as cutoff frequency; move left and right, and you're triggering another parameter, such as resonance. This app is known as the iTM Pad, shown in Figure 4.15.

iTM offers many other varieties, but one final one I'll mention is the iTM MCU, which stands for *Mackie Control Unit*. This application allows you to essentially control your mix and transport function of any DAW that supports Mackie control, such as Cubase, Pro Tools, or Logic Pro. This application essentially allows you to mix remotely from

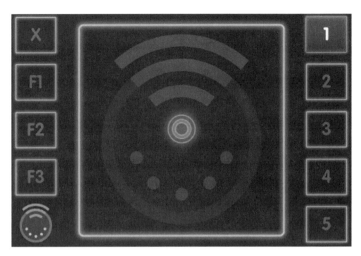

Figure 4.15   Control sound by moving your finger around the iTM Pad.

your iPhone or iPod Touch and start, stop, and record. It's perfect for the armchair producer or the engineer who is on the move around the studio.

In closing, I obviously had a lot of fun with the iTM products, but I will say that you definitely need to read the accompanying manuals to iTouchMidi, their Mac or PC application that allows these devices to work.

Having tested these apps on my MacBook Pro, I can certify that they work. And once they work, they are extremely helpful.

FiRe by Audiofile Engineering

If you've read one of my earlier books, *Creating Music and Sound for Games* (Course Technology PTR, 2006), you'll know that I'm a fan of field recording. And since the first release of the iPhone, I patiently waited for *the* field-recording app.

BIAS released one—didn't like it. Apple released one—didn't like it, and it was really buggy and caused me to lose a very important recording. SpeakEasy released one—actually used it a lot, but getting recordings from it was a little tough.

Finally, one day I was reading a music magazine and came across the FiRe recording app from Audiofile Engineering, and my prayers were answered. FiRe has everything I was looking for. It records in multiple formats, from Ogg Vorbis, to Broadcast WAV files, to AIFF—you name it. It provides multiple options for retrieving your audio recording from your iPod Touch or iPhone—through FTP (yes, it will load audio up to your FTP site for you) or through SoundCloud (if you have a SoundCloud account, anyway).

SoundCloud (www.soundcloud.com) is a paid service that takes the difficulty out of sharing and distributing audio files. There are multiple forms of memberships, each affording you different features, amount of storage, and so on. If you're an artist who wants to get your music out there and you don't really care for dealing with FTP sites and storage limits, this may be for you.

FiRe even gives you web access to what is on your Apple device. For example, when you enable browser access within FiRe, it generates a URL that you can go to and download your audio files, as shown in Figure 4.16.

Figure 4.16   Access your recordings from a custom website generated by your iPhone or iPod Touch with FiRe.

Beyond retrieval capabilities, Fire has a wonderful interface for use and recording. It has the big red Record button and the big green Play button. It generates waveforms during recording so that you can view what is happening, it displays the recording time prominently at the top of the screen so you can keep an eye on the length, and it has a meter directly below to ensure that you aren't peaking. See all of this in Figure 4.17.

Once the recording is finished, the playhead can be moved with the finger back to any point within the recording for reference.

Figure 4.17   FiRe has a minimal, to-the-point interface that anyone can pick up in a minute.

If you're concerned about the internal mic on your iPhone or iPod Touch, you can always go with a third-party microphone, such as the Blue Mikey, shown in Figure 4.18.

Figure 4.18   The Blue Mikey is a small microphone by an awesome manufacturer of pro mics. It fits right onto the bottom of your iPhone or iPod Touch.

Or, if you prefer to use your own microphone, you can always pick up an Alesis ProTrack, which has not only its own built-in stereo mic array, but also two XLR inputs. See Figure 4.19.

Figure 4.19   The Alesis ProTrack turns your iPhone or Touch into a handheld field recorder.

Finally, FiRe records in sample rates of 44.1 kHz, 22 kHz, and 11 kHz. No, there's no 96 kHz, but it's perfect for on-the-go recording!

As I mentioned in my previous book, field recording is a great way not only to expand on your library with original sounds, but also to capture moments that you can never get back aurally. And with FiRe's ability to add metadata onto each audio file recorded, you can document an awesome moment or a cool trick to get that one sound that makes the project.

Amidio Collection of Apps by Amidio

There are just some app creators out there that score a steady winning streak. However, it's not by luck, it's by carefully paying attention to what's out there, what's not out there, and what could be made better.

Amidio (www.amidio.com) is one of those developers. Being musicians, they have a good idea of what musicians want, and they make their apps the way musicians want them made: simple, flexible, and stable.

First, and one of my favorites in their collection, is Noise.io, shown in Figure 4.20, a full-fledged pro synthesizer for the iPhone and iPod Touch. When you fire it up for the first time, you may think that you are looking at something simple. Keep digging!

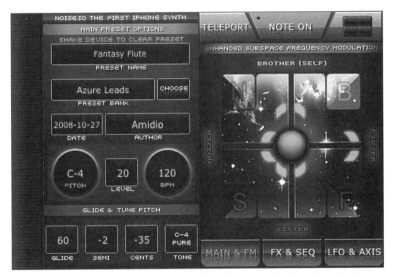

Figure 4.20   Noise.io is an amazingly robust synthesizer for the Apple touch devices that truly earns the ranking of pro.

In actuality, Noise.io features an extensive hybrid frequency modulation/subtractive synthesizer that is extremely editable. It also allows for tons of real-time manipulation with its KAOSS-style interface, and it's extremely simple to create cool, catchy melodies with its onboard sequencer (actually three, to be specific). This last statement, however, can be a little deceiving. While Noise.io does have sequencers built in, it is not a one-stop shop like BeatMaker, where you can create a whole song within it. It is what it claims to be: a synthesizer first and foremost, with some sequencing abilities—and it even has accelerometer support!

But it is a wonderfully complex and full-sounding synthesizer that would magnificently add inspiration and accompaniment to your existing DAW or outboard gear.

Amidio has also developed a very cool guitar app known as Star Guitar Pro (see Figure 4.21), a virtual guitarist wrapped up conveniently within your Apple tactile device. It's chock full of guitar loops, and you can easily find the chord you're looking for to add to any song you may be working on.

Figure 4.21   Star Guitar Pro is a full-fledged guitar accompaniment instrument for the iPhone/iPod Touch.

Now, before you scoff, think for a second. Imagine running this app through an amp simulator within Logic Pro or Native Instruments Guitar Rig. Imagine a little editing later on. For those of us who don't play guitar, this is a wonderful accompaniment for when we need guitar quickly, and it's currently only $4.99! Similar software that you may find out there, such as Steinberg's Virtual Guitarist 2, will run you around $199.99. And I'm not saying that the $4.99 iPhone/Touch app is better, but it's a very inexpensive building block should you have the need. Regardless, there's a very cool video of its performance with a vocalist at www.amidio.com/index.php/iphone-music-apps/star-guitar-pro.

Then there's the JR Hexatone Pro, a pinnacle edition to the Amidio lineup that makes music-making easy and fun. It's a six-directional drum machine and rhythm sequencer, as shown in Figure 4.22.

If my definition of this application comes off as confusing, trust me—I found the application a little confusing at first too. However, thanks to the wonderful Jordan Rudess walkthrough on their website, it began to click much more. And once I spent hours of time with it, it made even more sense.

Before going further, I should explain that Jordan Rudess is also the JR in JR Hexatone Pro. He is also the keyboardist for Dream Theater and the sound designer for JR

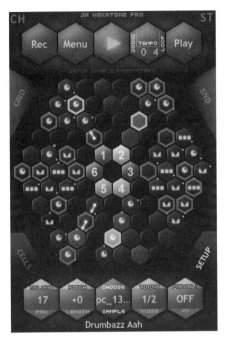

Figure 4.22   The JR Hexatone Pro is a truly unique rhythmic/melodic instrument for the iPhone that will not fail to inspire.

Hexatone Pro. The sound library boasts 400 samples; however, your own samples can be loaded into Hexatone Pro as well.

The Hexagon that you work within to make your rhythms and melodies is extremely inventive and offers a new and inspiring way to see all of your different parts playing at once. The Hexatone also features many different modifiers within the Hexagon work area that affect the playback of notes differently. For example, some modifiers may cause a note to stutter and so on.

Like other Amidio applications, the JR Hexatone Pro also takes advantage of the iPhone/ iPod Touch accelerometer. When enabled, you can cause stuttering and chorus effects to phase in with physical movements of your Apple device, making this a worthy live performance application.

But of all the features the JR Hexatone Pro sports, the one I've found to be the coolest is the randomization features of song and sound. You can actually have the JR Hexatone Pro create rhythmic patterns for you, as well as have it choose random samples.

This means that you could effectively sit there and have this small iPhone/iPod Touch application write parts for you while you record on your DAW. I mean, some people pay for rhythmic loops—you could have your portable device write them for you!

Conclusion to iPhone/iPod Touch Applications

Again, this short list has only been a glimpse of the applications that are available. But at the same time, I'm trying to give you current examples of what's out there. And while giving you a tour, I'm trying to give you ideas for using them with your current work, as standalone, for live performance, or for anything that you can think of.

Writing a comprehensive list would be a waste of time because it could change within minutes of writing this. These examples serve as stepping-stones toward thinking outside of the box and making your Apple portable device work for you in new and imaginative ways.

Now, let's talk a bit about some things to know about the iPhone and iPod Touch hardware.

iPhone/iPod Touch Pros and Cons

There's not much you can say against the current Apple lineup. They are solid, they seem to always be there when you need them, and they do everything! Yet, there are a few things I'd like to bring to your attention. Some of these you may already know; some of them may be new to you. But these are all in relation to our one true goal—music-making with these wonderful devices, the iPhone and iPod Touch, wherever you are. Let's start off by talking about the headphones.

Headphones

The iPhone headphones are extremely cool, and having them close by all the time ensures that you can really jam out and hear what you are doing, whether you're in the doctor's office, the train station, the airport, or wherever. I made a habit of carrying my headphones around in the little useless pocket found above the right pocket of my jeans, shown in Figure 4.23. I simply coil them up when I'm not using them and slide them into my pocket. If I need them, they are readily available. And yes, they do survive the washer in most cases.

If you don't like the iPhone standard headphones, there are tons of models from other companies besides Apple. Shure makes some in-ear headphones that are highly regarded and sound amazing. Shown in Figure 4.24, the Shure headphones fit snugly inside the ear and pretty much cancel out any outside noise.

One thing to note, though: If you are one of those people, like me, who use the headphones for telephone calls as well, these headphones do not have a built-in microphone. Shure does make an adapter called the MPA-3C, shown in Figure 4.25, that adds a button and microphone like the original Apple iPhone headphones. It also increases the overall length of the cable.

Figure 4.23   The Shure headphones sound wonderful and block out any unwanted noise, period.

Figure 4.24   The Shure MPA-3C is a really cool adapter that adds a microphone to any headset.

If you're using an iPod Touch, headphones can pretty much be anything you want. However, remember that the iPod Touch supports a mic too, for things such as Skype and even music applications like I Am T-Pain, which allows you to sing along with beats with real Antares Auto-Tune technology.

Outputs

While the headphones are wonderful on the go, when you're utilizing the iPhone/Touch in the studio, the built-in speaker is not going to cut it. And like the Nintendo DS, you

Figure 4.25   Alesis makes a wonderful line of mixers that use the iPod Classic as the recording device.

can run a 1/8-inch-stereo-to-1/8-inch-stereo cable to your laptop's audio input, or you could pick up a 1/8-inch-stereo-to-dual-1/4-inch cable to your audio interface. For pictures of both cables, see Chapter 2's section on Nintendo DS outputs.

The iPhone and Touch also have an additional option—the same port at the bottom that you use to charge your device, connect to your computer, and so on can utilize specialized cables and accessories that expand your outputs.

I briefly mentioned the Composite AV Cable from Apple earlier in this chapter. This cable will not only charge your device, but it will also allow you to watch movies from your Phone/Touch on a television. But, I've found you can also use the white and red jacks to be used for output on any iPhone/Touch applications. Simply get a couple of RCA-to-1/4-inch connectors, and you can connect directly to most audio interfaces.

If you're using an iPod Classic, you may be interested in knowing that Alesis, longtime audio manufacturers, have also created small mixing desks that allow you to mix down directly to your iPod (see Figure 4.25). These are awesome if you're someone who would prefer to avoid the computer altogether. You're provided with aux sends, returns, three-band EQs on each channel, onboard digital effects, and more.

If you're a DJ, you'll be happy to know that there are a number of devices, ranging in price, that allow you to use the iPhone, iPod Classic, iPod Touch, and so on within a small DJ mixer encasement. Urban Outfitters, normally known for clothes, is strangely a source for a DJ mixer that supports not only the iPod line, but the iPhone as well (see Figure 4.26).

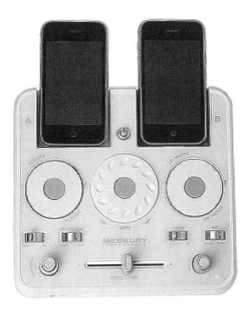

Figure 4.26   Use your iPhone, iPod Touch, or iPod Classic to DJ.

Airplane Mode and the iPhone

If the iPhone is your main axe, it is vital that you remember to enable Airplane Mode during performances, sessions, and so on. There's nothing worse than capturing some cool amalgamation of sound that you've spent some time on, only to have a call come in and completely destroy the moment. Furthermore, some applications don't hold onto your work when a call comes in—they will simply return to default sounds, rhythms, and so on.

So, if you're in the middle of making some music with your iPhone and you're in a sensitive position with your creation—that is, you like what's happening, but you haven't saved yet—save and go into Airplane Mode. This will be especially important to do for the next chapter, where we'll be doing exercises within BeatMaker.

Airplane Mode can be enabled by touching Settings and then sliding the switch to On. See Figure 4.27.

Figure 4.27   Remember to save often and enable Airplane Mode when making music on the iPhone.

Conclusion

We've covered some amazing apps in this chapter and talked about some important factors regarding the iPhone and iPod Touch that should have you raring to go in terms of making music, experimenting with sound, and having some simple audio fun. In the next chapter, we'll explore BeatMaker for the iPhone in depth so that you can get an idea of how far you can really go with one of the most elaborate audio apps for the iPhone.

5 BeatMaker

There are some applications that you find out about through a friend, and you fall in love with them because they make your life easier, because they inspire you creatively, or because of a slew of other reasons. There are some applications that you find looking around the Apple App Store, and you decide to give them a shot.

There are some applications that you hear about in development way before they appear on the market, and upon reading about said application, you say to yourself, "This is the one for me."

That is how I felt about BeatMaker, shown in Figure 5.1, weeks before its arrival in the App Store. I got giddy when I saw pictures of the virtual FX processors and the small drum machine–styled pads. I salivated over the built-in wave editor for editing your own samples—this was what I'd been waiting for.

When I finally got my hands on BeatMaker, it didn't disappoint me. It did everything I wanted. It gave me a way to compose on the iPhone when I was out and about. It gave me the ability to arrange; it gave me the ability to sample.

BeatMaker did cause me some disappointment in one respect, however. It caused me to disappoint myself.

How? I disappointed myself in failing to spend the time to really learn it and get to know it at first. Let's face it; there are so many apps out there that it's really easy to get in that sad habit of buying without ever really utilizing the tools you've purchased.

I've since spent time getting to know, use, and love BeatMaker. And the whole point of this chapter is to help you learn it fully, so that it's not a wasted purchase. This chapter is a primer to inspire you to try out an app that is truly worth your time—from the inspired community at Intua.net, to the large amounts of BeatMaker kits (sounds), to the beautiful graphical user interface that will make you feel right at home.

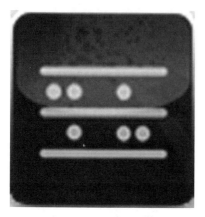

Figure 5.1 BeatMaker is an amazing application that allows you not only to tap your beats in on virtual pads, but also to arrange and create full songs.

Before beginning our tour of BeatMaker, if you are on an iPhone, I'd advise you to put the phone in Airplane Mode. To do this, go to Settings on your iPhone. The very first option is Airplane Mode. Put the switch in the On position. If you are expecting a call, you may want to do this tour later, because Airplane Mode will turn off the phone portion of the iPhone.

Getting to Know BeatMaker

BeatMaker is made up of four main sections that all work together in a big way. I'll describe them in the following sections.

The Homepage

The homepage is an informational page that also serves as your load and save page for sounds, kits, and so on. What I think is particularly cool about the homepage is that it acts sort of like a web browser that has initial instructions for using BeatMaker, news, and so on. This way, you can always be up to date on what the developer (Intua) has available for you. I also think it's cool that they have really big buttons for Load, Save Project, Export, and Save Kit, as shown in Figure 5.2. There are too many manufacturers that would rather make these highly important features hidden in the background so that they don't spoil the GUI. BeatMaker has them as soon as you're completely booted into the program. This completely gels with the regular workflow for most. Think about it: You boot up the program, you load the project or load a kit, and then you move on to the other parts.

The Pads Screen

The Pads screen (see Figure 5.3) is not only where you can play your beats, sounds, and so on, it's also where you can fine-tune sounds, record samples, and work with the levels of

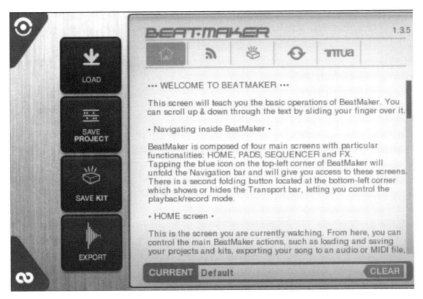

Figure 5.2 The homepage is not only an informational page about all things BeatMaker; it's also a place to load and save projects and kits.

each individual drum sound. There is even a wave editor found in the Pads screen where you can do some minor editing of sounds that currently exist within your kit or edit audio that you brought in with the Audio screen (also found within the Pads screen) that allows you to record audio for use with a pad, just like the sampling drum machines of old.

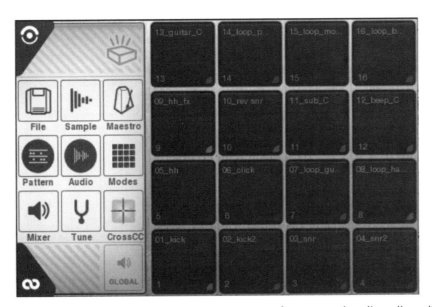

Figure 5.3 The Pads screen is where you can perform, record audio, edit audio, mix individual kit sounds, and more.

The Sequencer Screen

If you're familiar with desktop sequencing applications, such as Pro Tools, Cubase, Logic Pro, and so on, then the Sequencer screen will most likely seem very familiar to you. And indeed it should—BeatMaker gives you the best of desktop MIDI sequencing in this section. Here you can add loops that you've created in the Pads screen, or you can create a brand-new loop by step editing. The step editors, velocity, pan, groove, and tune all allow you to fine-tune your patterns. Tune, for example, lets you make melodies where the Pads screen can't—unless of course you have various samples of an instrument in different keys. The Sequencer screen also has well-known commands such as Insert Bar, Remove Bar, and so on—things you've come to expect from all sequencers.

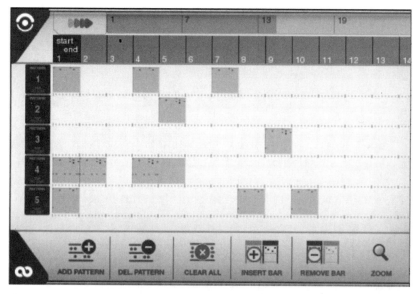

Figure 5.4 Use the Sequencer screen to arrange your song, create melodies, and more.

The FX Screen

If you've read my other books, you know I'm a big fan of and have a long history with Reason from Propellerhead (www.propellerheads.se). The FX screen, like Reason, has several small "hardware-esque" FX devices stacked in a "rack." The rack is composed of a 3-band EQ, shown in Figure 5.5.

It also has a synchronized digital delay (see Figure 5.6).

And there's a killer-sounding BitCrusher for making parts of your pattern sound grungy, lo-fi, or just straight dirty (see Figure 5.7).

And finally, there's a wonderful Filter module supplying you with High-Pass, Low-Pass, and Band-Pass modes (see Figure 5.8).

Figure 5.5   BeatMaker has a 3-band EQ.

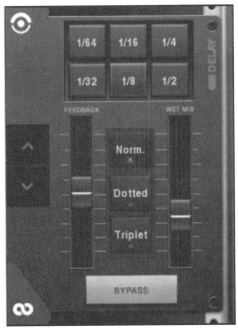

Figure 5.6   Make some killer delayed patterns with BeatMaker's digital delay.

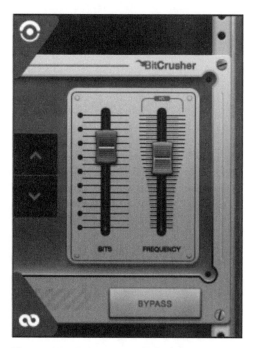

Figure 5.7   Bring some digital dirt into your song with BeatMaker's BitCrusher.

Figure 5.8   Bring some sweeps and separation into your mix with BeatMaker's Filter.

Although the FX are cool and sound amazing for a mobile device, remember that you can only do so much with them. For example, you cannot automate any FX data. But you do get two racks of FX, both carrying one of each FX device mentioned previously. BeatMaker gives you routing capabilities where one sample (or pad within the Pads screen) can be routed to one FX rack, and another sample on another pad is routed to another rack. And finally, you can have a set of samples that are simply dry coming out of the main mix.

If the FX units in BeatMaker can't be automated, what good are they? Well, you can adjust a setting on an FX unit like an EQ or filter as you would in GarageBand or Pro Tools, where the sound "stays" at that setting throughout the song. Although it may not sound fun right off the bat, if you think about it, there are many EQ settings, delay settings, or distortion settings that stay at the same setting throughout most songs.

One thing you might consider is that you *can* change settings while your BeatMaker song is playing in real time for a live performance or while you're recording in real time into your computer or audio interface. Live FX changes can add real spice and spontaneity to a recording or show!

Pattern/Song Creation in BeatMaker

The capabilities are there in BeatMaker, as you can see. We have everything we need to create a cool track, with only a couple minor limitations: a small screen and not every option in our usual DAW of choice. But remember, this is a portable device! We can be recording, creating, and producing wherever we go!

If you think about it, compared to a computer, a guitar is more or less a one-trick pony. It plays one sound that can, of course, be modified through FX, amps, and so on, but in the end it will still sound like a guitar! Kind of limited, don't you think? Not really! The limitations of a guitar aren't really limitations. It does something wonderful that no other instrument does as well. It excels at being a guitar. And many, many songs have been written on just a guitar—perhaps more than any other instrument out there—and have gone on to amass fame and fortune for the songwriter.

When most of us evaluate software, especially in these rapidly changing modern times, we are quick to write off a piece of software or a software instrument because it doesn't do everything we want it to. However, take a minute to see what it excels at before you pass on a device. You may find a new irreplaceable instrument that goes on to be a sonic muse for your next big hit!

In this section, we'll go over pattern creation, editing, and recording audio, all the way up to song creation. It is helpful if you currently own BeatMaker, but it's not necessary. I'll be layering in tips for portable devices throughout this section, so even if you don't own BeatMaker, there are still little gems to be found. Pay close attention to the notes, too! These transcend far beyond iPhones into general tips for recording, performing, and, above all, inspiration! If you like, consider it a journal of someone noting how they are using an iPhone to create music. Also, don't forget to put on your headphones or plug your Apple device into some speakers. If you don't know how, see Chapter 6 for iPhone studio integration.

Loading Your Kit

After I choose BeatMaker from my iPhone desktop by simply pressing the BeatMaker icon shown in Figure 5.9, a loading screen appears, and then eventually the homepage shown in Figure 5.10 appears.

Figure 5.9   Press the BeatMaker icon on your desktop.

The first thing I do once I'm inside BeatMaker is load a kit. To do this, I press the Load button shown in Figure 5.11.

In BeatMaker, you can load up sets of drum pads that are already assigned sounds, or samples. The sets of pads have already been edited, mixed, and fine-tuned. These sets are known as *kits* in BeatMaker terminology.

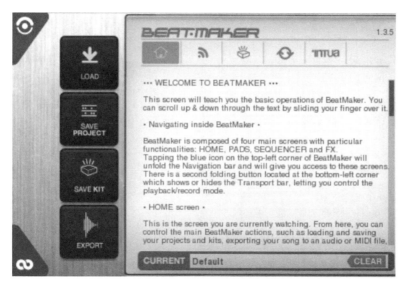

Figure 5.10   After a few seconds of loading, the homepage will appear.

Figure 5.11   Press the Load button.

In the Load menu, I'm presented three menu options: Artists Kits, BeatMaker Soundbank, and My Content, also shown in Figure 5.12.

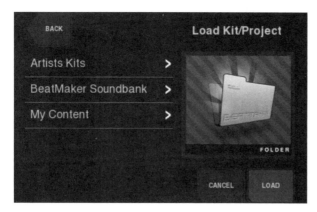

Figure 5.12   The Load menu.

Artists Kits are stylized kits created by various artists that you may or may not have heard of. There's also My Content—this area is the path back to kits you've created, projects (also known as songs), recordings, and exports (recorded versions of songs created in BeatMaker).

For demonstration purposes, I'll choose BeatMaker Soundbank. This menu is filled with kits based on genre, such as rock, hip-hop, and electronica (see Figure 5.13).

Figure 5.13   The BeatMaker Soundbank is filled with kits organized by genre.

Inside the BeatMaker Soundbank menu, I'll choose the Hip-Hop category by flicking my thumb forward to see it and then pressing where it says Hip-Hop. See Figure 5.14.

Figure 5.14   Scroll down to where you see Hip-Hop and press the words.

Upon tapping Hip-Hop, I'm given two options for kits—Battle Hop and Old School Hip-Hop. Being a former soldier, I'll choose Battle Hop, then Battle Hop.bmk, and then press the Load button (see Figure 5.15).

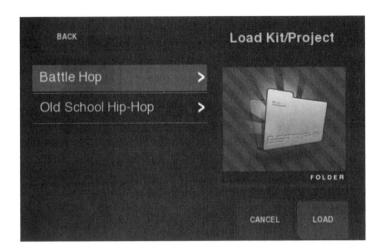

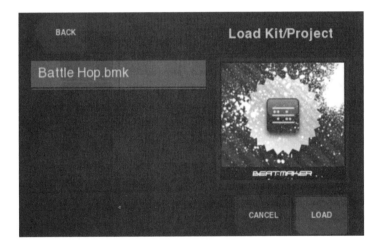

Figure 5.15   Choose Battle Hop, then Battle Hop.bmk, and then Load.

Immediately, I'm greeted with a loading screen, and then I'm left back at the homepage. Where are the pads?!

In the upper-right corner of all of the BeatMaker screens, you'll notice a small blue button, also shown in Figure 5.16.

Figure 5.16   Press the Menu button.

This Menu button opens a small menu at the top of BeatMaker that allows you to move from screen to screen. Notice sections we've already talked about: Home, Pads, Sequencer, FX. See Figure 5.17.

Figure 5.17   The menu bar in BeatMaker.

I'll press the Pads button, shown in Figure 5.17, and now I can see the pads that make BeatMaker famous, shown in Figure 5.18.

Take a moment to play around with the pads. Check out the different sounds and notice that some pads trigger loops. Try playing a beat in real time with just your fingers—this is a great way to get some inspiration for recording. Sometimes just playing a simple beat will trigger your brain to start coming up with other parts, such as melodies and lyrics.

Have some fun, and when you're ready, move to the next section to learn how to record a pattern!

Recording a Pattern

Though you can create patterns in the Sequencer screen, it's much more fun in the Pads screen. I say this because the Pads screen has the pads, the pads allow more interaction with playback, and that makes it fun. The Sequencer screen requires more manual entry, which is great for some. I like to play, though.

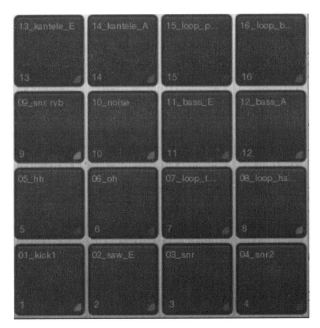

Figure 5.18   The BeatMaker drum pads!

In the lower-left corner of the screen, you'll notice that there is another button in Beat-Maker that is always there (see Figure 5.19).

Figure 5.19   Press this button to trigger the transport bar.

This button is for the transport bar. This particular type of command strip can be found in any sequencing application. What is it? It allows you to play your beat, stop your beat, record your beat, and loop your beat. And, in the Sequencer screen, it does the same thing. See Figure 5.20.

Figure 5.20   The transport bar allows you to play your project, record in your project, and so on.

It is important to note that this bar does not record audio; it only records beats. Audio is recorded in the Pads screen, but we will be getting to this later in this chapter. See the section called "Recording Audio for Your Pattern/Kit."

After I bring up my transport bar, I press the Record button. Immediately, I hear a click track, and if I look again at the transport bar, I'll notice that indeed the Metronome button, shown in Figure 5.21, has lit up green. By default, the click track always goes on when you start recording.

Figure 5.21   The Metronome will automatically start up when you press Record.

You'll also notice on the transport bar that the Loop button (see Figure 5.22) is slightly gray, signifying that it is pressed as well. This is perfect, because if I start playing a beat now, it will automatically loop back whatever I play.

Figure 5.22   By default, BeatMaker will always turn on Loop when you start recording.

Now that I'm recording and my Metronome (also known as a click track; see the following note) is playing, I'll start tapping a beat along with the click track. Something simple, such as a kick and a snare . . . Try it yourself, but keep it simple—just a little bit at a time! See Figure 5.23.

A click track, or metronome, gives you an audible reference for how fast your sequencer—in this case, BeatMaker—is recording and playing back. If you are recording a beat in a sequencing application, it's helpful to record along with the click. Otherwise, your beat will be out of time, or if Quantization is enabled, it will sound completely different from what you actually played. Quantization is explained next, so keep reading.

Figure 5.23   I start tapping my beat along with the click track in BeatMaker.

Notice that as the playback loops back around, the timing appears to be corrected. No, you're not just *that* good of a drummer on a small portable device! The timing is much smoother due to an underlying process known as *quantization* that is also enabled by default.

> Recording beats accurately on a small handheld device is almost impossible for many reasons, especially with parts such as hi-hats, where multiple beats are triggered swiftly and any off timing is immediately heard. BeatMaker, like many sequencing applications, has a feature known as Quantization that attempts to correct the timing of anything played into it. It does this by slightly moving notes over to the appropriate beat within the guidelines of a sequencer and its set Quantize resolution. The resolutions of a Quantize function are set up as particular kinds of notes, such as like sixteenth notes, eighth notes, and so on. The most common resolution for pop, hip-hop, and so on is a sixteenth note. Above all, quantization functions keep us sounding polished and pro!

If the timing sounds completely different from what you originally played, you may want to change the Quantize mode to a different setting. You can do this by pressing the Pattern button and then pressing the arrow up button until it shows the quantization resolutions available for BeatMaker. You can even disable the Quantization feature by pressing the Off button. See Figure 5.24.

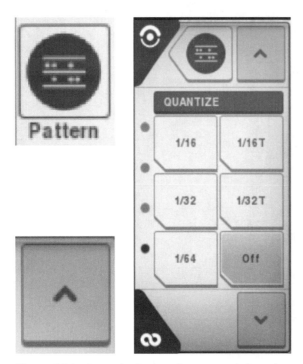

Figure 5.24   Press the Pattern button and then the up arrow to get to the Quantize page. If you want to disable quantization, press the Off button on this page.

If you decide that you want to move on to the next pattern after recording this one, press the up arrow again until it says Pattern 1, as shown in Figure 5.25. This screen allows you to move to a new pattern from within the Pads screen, while still jamming along with what you've already done. Each new pattern will automatically be assigned a lane within the Sequencer window, which I'll show later.

To move to the next pattern, press the New button on this screen, as shown in Figure 5.25.

When you press the New button, you will notice that what once said Pattern 1 now says Pattern 2. You will also notice that you still hear your original loop in the background. BeatMaker does this as a convenience so that you have something to groove along to. It is possible to go to the Sequencer page and turn off this loop, but really, you can use this to your advantage.

When I start with Pattern 1, I will simply play one to two pads, nothing more—usually kick and snare. When I switch to the second pattern, I will add hi-hat. Third will be bass, and down the line. Once I get to the Sequencer page, I can determine when each pattern will play and essentially layer each part to form a song. If this doesn't make sense now, don't worry—it will when we get to the Sequencer page.

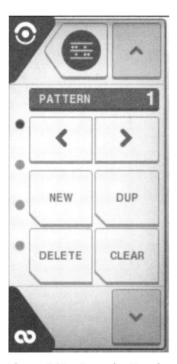

Figure 5.25   Press the New button to start a new pattern. Keep in mind that your first loop will play handily in the background.

Try out what I mentioned in the previous note, adding just a few pads in a layer at a time. It's fun, and in the next section, we'll check out the Sequencer page to see how it all works together.

If you want to delete your first pattern to try this, simply press the Delete button on this page. See Figure 5.26.

Figure 5.26   Press the Delete button to delete your work if you need to.

Pattern Arrangement in the Sequencer

Press the button in the upper-left corner of the screen to access the menu bar and then select Sequencer. You'll instantly be greeted with a familiar sight (if you have used other music applications): multiple lanes for arranging parts within a song. Look at Figure 5.27 to see what I'm talking about.

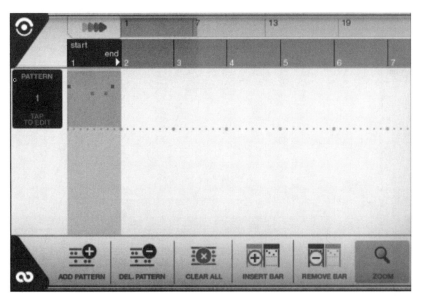

Figure 5.27   The Sequencer page is a familiar sight to those who have worked with most DAW applications.

Though familiar, this sequencer is still a bit different. Whereas GarageBand, Pro Tools, or Logic simply lets you start recording for as long as you want, this sequencer only allows you to arrange patterns that you create in the Pattern page or through step editing in the Sequencer page.

At this moment, I have about four patterns in my Sequencer page. You can tell that they are patterns by the colorful objects (notes) within a small blocked area (measure). See Figure 5.28.

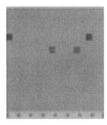

Figure 5.28   Patterns appear in the Sequencer page as small blocks with colors inside of them. These colored specks are notes; the blocks are measures.

By clicking in the empty area of a pattern lane, I can add a new instance of a pattern, as shown in Figure 5.29.

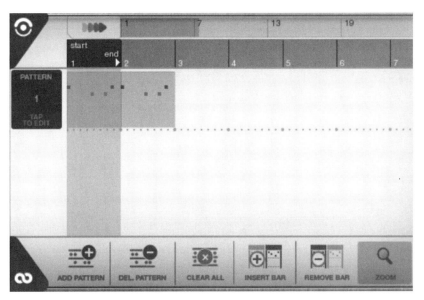

Figure 5.29   Click in the empty area of a pattern lane to add a new pattern instance.

Or, by touching an existing pattern instance, I can get rid of a pattern instance, as shown in Figure 5.30.

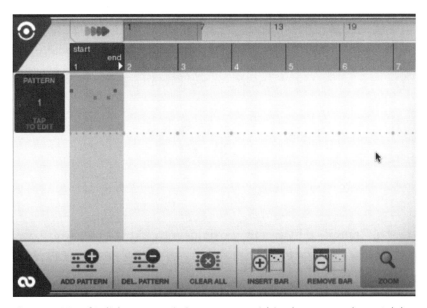

Figure 5.30   If I click on an existing pattern within the pattern lane, I delete only that instance of the pattern.

What's also cool is that anywhere within the pattern lane I press, a new instance appears. This makes it easy to spread parts around and arrange. In this example, I'll make a pattern appear every other measure by tapping every other measure. See Figure 5.31.

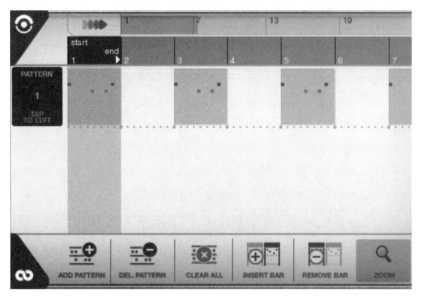

Figure 5.31   Patterns now appear at every other measure.

At the bottom of the screen, there are familiar commands such as Insert Bar, Remove Bar, and Zoom, shown in Figure 5.32.

Figure 5.32   The Sequencer page has familiar commands for old-time DAW users.

You can use the Remove Bar command by simply moving your right loop locator to the beginning of the bar that you want to delete by tapping the desired bar and then pressing Remove Bar to get rid it. You can tap Insert Bar to add a bar directly to the right of the playback head. See Figure 5.33. It's also important to note that if you drag within the loop locator field, you increase the length of the loop. To enable looping, simply press the Loop button in the transport bar on the bottom.

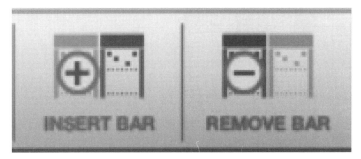

Figure 5.33   Move the loop locator before whichever measure you want to get rid of by tapping the desired measure, and then press Remove Bar to remove a bar from your composition or Insert Bar to add a bar to your composition.

There are even buttons such as Add Pattern, which will create a new pattern lane with nothing in it at the bottom of the screen, and Delete Pattern, which allows you to simply press a pattern lane that you don't want and remove it altogether.

But wait, the Sequencer does even more! Let's talk about pattern editing within the Sequencer page.

Pattern Editing

Notice that at the beginning of every pattern lane, there is a button that says Pattern <Number> Tap to Edit, as shown in Figure 5.34.

Figure 5.34   Tap here to go to the Pattern Editor.

This button allows you to access the pattern editing functions and Step Editors that are so powerful in many DAW applications. I'll add that this is another way to create patterns if the pads in the Pads screen are too small for your fingers.

When you initially tap the Tap to Edit button, you'll see a window very similar to the Piano Roll Editor in Logic. This allows you to create and delete notes by simply tapping on one of the colored fields. See Figure 5.35.

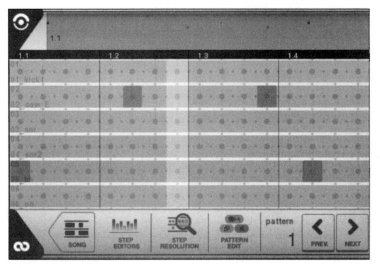

Figure 5.35   The Pattern Editor is similar to the Piano Roll mode in Logic and many other pattern editors in other DAWs. It lets you manually enter and delete notes by tapping in the lanes.

The Pattern Editor is also intensely valuable when used with the Pads screen. Imagine making this killer pattern, but there's one beat that is off—if you could fix it, it would be perfect! That's what the Pattern Editor is for: Edit the pattern, find the note, and delete it. Then, add it where you want it to go.

You can also access the Step Editors within the Pattern Editor by pressing the Step Editors button, as shown in Figure 5.36.

Figure 5.36   Press the Step Editors button to access the Step Editors within BeatMaker.

These modes allow you to modify essentials, such as the pitch of an individual note, the groove, the beat, and so on. You can even adjust the velocity or pan of any particular note, adding subtlety, polish, and spaciousness to your pattern. See the menu bar for the Step Editors, shown in Figure 5.37.

Figure 5.37 The menu bar for the Step Editors.

It's important to note that the Step Editors work slightly differently than the Pattern Editor. Whereas the Pattern Editor lets you place notes, the Step Editors modify how the note is played. For example, when I go into the Pitch Editor by pressing the button shown in Figure 5.37, I only see a grid with some columns that are colored a little darker, as shown in Figure 5.38.

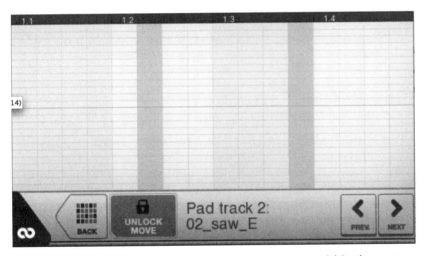

Figure 5.38 The darker columns indicate existing notes within the pattern.

These darker columns indicate that this is actually a note or beat that is being used. If I click up or down within the column, as shown in Figure 5.39, I raise or lower the pitch of this beat.

What's handy about changing the pitch? Let's say you have a recorded note of a bass guitar in your BeatMaker kit. Normally, this note plays the same the whole way through a pattern. With the Pitch Editor, you can actually make a bass melody by changing the pitch of different notes within the pattern. Suddenly, BeatMaker is more than a beat-maker; it's now a melody-maker.

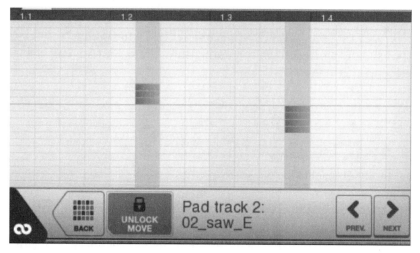

Figure 5.39 Pressing up or down within the darkened column allows me to change the pitch of the beat associated with this column.

I highly suggest playing around with the Step Editors. They offer a great way to refine and individualize your patterns. And, they offer a chance at true inspiration and creativity while away from the studio.

Recording Audio for Your Pattern/Kit

One of the reasons why I chose to highlight BeatMaker for this book is that it offers almost everything that a standard DAW such as Pro Tools has—even down to the ability to record within your project on the go.

Granted, there are many applications out there for the Apple portable devices that allow you to do multitrack recording. But this application allows you to record and then immediately place the recorded file in with programmed melodies and drums.

This is particularly inspirational in that you can sing in vocal ideas and then play with how they would be triggered within a drum pattern. Or, you record multiple sounds around you within an environment, such as a bottle crash or a trashcan lid, and make those impact sounds a part of your kit. And, you can even share the kit with a friend later or export a loop created with said kit to your DAW—the potential is staggering. And it's all from your phone, on the go.

In this section, I'd like to show you how to record your own audio within BeatMaker, and then I'll show you how to edit it.

First, click the button in the upper-right corner to trigger the menu bar and choose the Pads button. See Figure 5.40.

Figure 5.40 Bring up the menu bar and press the Pads button.

Next press the Audio button, as shown in Figure 5.41.

Figure 5.41 Press the Audio button.

The very first screen that appears when you press the Audio button is the Audio Recording page. You'll notice that prominently in the middle of the small page on the left is the Record Now button. And at the bottom, there's a simple Select button to choose which pad you want to record to. See Figure 5.42.

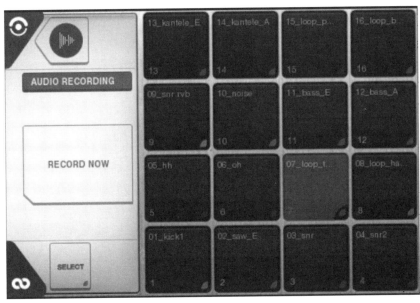

Figure 5.42 It's easy to use this page. There's a big Record Now button and a place to select which pad you want to record on to.

I've noticed that the Select button on my version of BeatMaker does nothing at all. Perhaps this will be fixed in later versions. I simply had to press a pad without pressing the Select button; it was enough to indicate where BeatMaker should record.

If you press the pad that you want to record over and press the Record Now button, BeatMaker will start recording, as shown in Figure 5.43. It is important to note that you cannot hear anything else while recording, not even a click track. Hopefully, they will make this an option in future versions, when headphones are connected, and so on.

Figure 5.43 Press the Record Now button, and it starts recording.

For the purposes of getting that quick percussion hit or just laying down a cool vocal line, this will do the trick. When you've finished recording, press the Stop button, shown in Figure 5.44.

Figure 5.44 Press the Stop button to stop recording.

When you do this, you'll be greeted by the Edit button along with Save, Cancel, and Listen (see Figure 5.45).

Figure 5.45 When you finish recording audio, BeatMaker will ask you whether you want to Save, Cancel, Edit, or Listen.

By choosing Cancel, you're telling BeatMaker, "Whoops, changed my mind. I don't want to replace the recording that was on this pad with my new one." At that point, the original pad recording stays. Pressing Save tells BeatMaker that you want to name this recording, while also keeping it within this kit, on the previously selected pad.

But before I save, I'm going to do a little editing to clean up my recording.

Figure 5.46 shows the Editing screen. A large waveform display is given to you, and you are allowed to use your fingers to move the beginning and end points (the thin lines on both sides of the recording) to the beginning and the end of where you want the recording to actually play back.

For triggered recordings, especially recordings that are intended as percussive, it's important to get the start point as close as possible to the beginning of the hit without cutting off part of the sound.

To help with this, BeatMaker's Sample Editor has two sets of Zoom buttons that appear as + and −, also shown in Figure 5.46. To the left, shown in Figure 5.47, there are also buttons that allow you to modify how the start and stop points work for editing.

Although the Editor is extremely simple compared to many other wave editing applications for the Apple devices, it's effective for this application. As I mentioned previously,

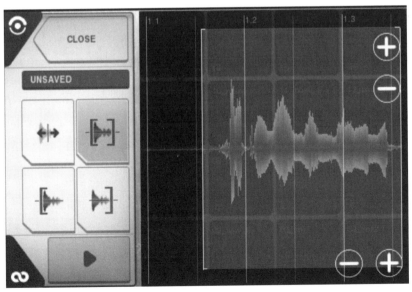

Figure 5.46 The Editing screen of BeatMaker not only shows you a waveform for your editing needs, but it also provides beginning and ending points that can be moved with your fingers and zoom buttons to get some tight edits on your recording.

I hope they'll expand its capabilities in the future. But this is the beauty of the App Store platform—developers can update an application at any minute.

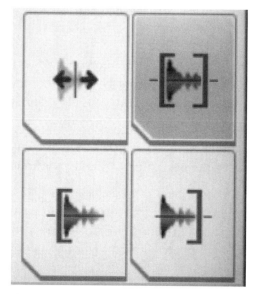

Figure 5.47   These buttons allow you to change the way the start and stop positions move within the Editor.

Next, let's talk about FX.

FX

The FX screen in BeatMaker can be confusing at first, but once you've figured it out, it's quite simple. I'm going to stay in the Pads screen and select Mixer from the initial menu; see Figure 5.48.

Figure 5.48   Press the Mixer button.

Next, I'll press the up arrow so that I move to the page labeled Output Bus. See Figure 5.49.

Figure 5.49 Press the up arrow so that you are placed in a screen titled Output Bus.

If you look closely at Figure 5.49, you'll notice that it's a very simple screen with three buttons: Main, FX 1, and FX 2. If I click the Select button at the bottom and tap three different pads, they will all highlight with a white hue (see Figure 5.50).

Figure 5.50 Press the Select button and tap each pad that you want to select and then press FX 2.

Once they are highlighted, I can tap FX 2, and they will all be assigned to FX 2. This will work the same for FX 1 and Master. However, anything that is tagged as Master will not be affected by the FX processors within BeatMaker.

Next, I'll select a few different pads to go through FX 1. See Figure 5.51.

Figure 5.51   Press the Select button and tap each pad that you want to select and then press FX 1.

Now, I'll activate the page bar in the upper-right corner and choose FX (see Figure 5.52).

Figure 5.52   Go to the FX page.

The FX page by default will display two delay units side by side, as shown in Figure 5.53. Don't be fooled, though—there are other FX devices as well. The delay unit is a simple effect that makes whatever signal is routed through it echo.

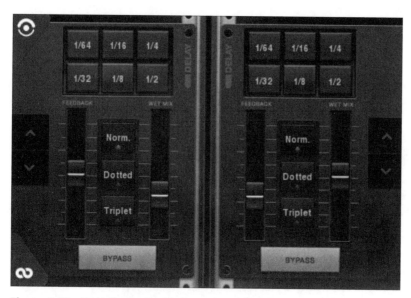

Figure 5.53   By default, you'll always see the delay units first.

Additional FX units can be accessed by pressing the up and down arrows on the far right and far left of each FX device. See Figure 5.54.

Figure 5.54 The arrows let you toggle between different FX units.

But before we move on, let's tie this together with what we did in the Output page earlier. The FX unit on the left, within the FX Screen, is FX 1; anything we routed into FX 1 will go through this device. The FX unit on the right is, as you might have guessed, FX 2. See Figure 5.55.

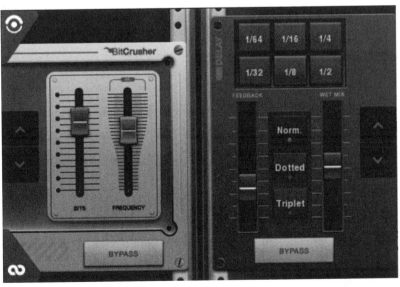

Figure 5.55 The left unit affects FX 1 routed signals; the right affects FX 2 routed signals.

Main does not go through either of these units and will not be affected by anything you do with them.

One thing to note: If you were to try tweaking any knobs on either of these devices while your audio is playing (by simply pressing Play in the transport bar), nothing would happen. They would be empty slider movements made possible by moving your fingers around.

If you pressed the Bypass button in Figure 5.56, which is always green by default, you would hear some FX.

Figure 5.56   The Bypass button, when green, essentially turns off the FX or bypasses them.

Although this isn't necessarily what *bypass* means regularly, Bypass essentially turns off the FX units, or allows sound to go through them without adding any FX. If Bypass is on (green), it means that sound is going through without any FX. If it's gray, sound is going through with FX.

It's possible to keep one FX unit in Bypass, while having two or more running FX at the same time. For example, if you press the Bypass button on the delay unit so that it's gray and then press the arrow down and go to the EQ, shown in Figure 5.57, and press the Bypass button on this unit so that it's gray, both units will be actively affecting audio at the same time.

Figure 5.57   The EQ FX unit allows you to trim or boost high, low, or medium frequencies out of audio.

It's also possible to have FX 1 and FX 2 going at the same time, allowing you to affect different busses (FX 1 and FX 2) simultaneously but in different combinations. For example, your hi-hat might have delay from FX 1, and your kick might have a boosted low end from the EQ in FX 2.

Because FX modifications can be done in real time, it is possible to perform some very cool adjustments in real time that will impress anyone who listens to you as you work.

Conclusion

Believe it, or not, we've only covered a portion of what BeatMaker can actually do. This chapter is only meant to be a helpful walkthrough to whet your appetite and give you some ideas on how you could utilize BeatMaker within your own work. It's also meant to be an in-depth look at the brilliant quality that's out there for instant download, which can be immediately accessed from your pocket. I would encourage you to explore BeatMaker more, but you may also find another app out there that does this and more. The important thing is that you can now see what's possible.

Should you decide to invest in BeatMaker, know that it has an extremely in-depth manual available at www.intua.net. Also know that the company is always adding new features, so if something doesn't jive in this walkthrough, check the manual—it has probably changed since I wrote this at version 1.3.4.

In the next chapter, we will investigate BeatMaker a little more, along with some other applications, in order to learn how to get audio from portable devices into your computer.

6 Handheld Studio Integration Part 1

One thing I've always noticed is that despite all the innovations made by the developers who've created some of the amazing software we've covered in this book, they are largely unrecognized by the manufacturers of handheld devices.

And that's okay. Crafty musicians throughout time have found new ways to use objects to make music, dating back to the nomadic days when all they had were drums. I mean, do you honestly think calfskin was designed to be laid across a cylinder of wood and tied tightly so that it would make a beat? No, it was designed as a layer of flesh to keep an animal's organs contained! But musicians always find a way.

And I think that's part of the fun—looking for new ways to be creative, new sounds, and new avenues of self expression.

At this point, if you've been paying attention to what you've been reading, you've learned that the current offerings of mobile devices are extremely powerful calfskin drums. Like the nomads, you can take these portable devices with you wherever you go and be a musician.

This chapter and the next focus on bringing your handheld device (or calfskin drum) back to the studio. They offer ideas for how to get what you've created from your mobile device (or devices) to your computer and ideas for how to capture what you create in real time with your handheld devices.

As we move forward, I've written these next two chapters so that they essentially work with any portable device. This way, if there's a particular device that wasn't covered in this book (or that was created after this book was written), you can still have some fun. As such, as we move through these chapters, unless I specify a particular device, such as a Nintendo DS or an iPod Touch, know that I'm referring to all mobile devices.

What makes these next chapters so important is the simple fact that when you get right down to it, handheld devices such as the Nintendo DS, the iPhone, and so on were not made with the musician in mind. If you want to use them for music, at some point you have to get creative with routing, recording, and so on. These chapters encompass the methods I've used for creation and capture with a computer, the hands-down main component of any studio at this juncture.

In these chapters we'll cover synchronization methods to lock tempos between the handheld device and the computer. We'll also talk about recording methods for handheld devices, so that you can get the best sound out of your mobile compositions and loops. And finally, we'll cover creative ways to use a handheld device that make recording fun and new again.

But before we get going, let's take a minute to go over connections again. After all, we have to connect to the computer somehow, right?

Connecting Your Handheld to Your Computer (Reprise)

I've mentioned adapters for particular devices in previous chapters, but before I move forward, let's just make sure we're clear for this chapter on which adapters you'll need.

If You're Using an Audio Interface

If you're using an audio interface, such as a Digidesign/Avid Mbox 2, PreSonus FP10, and so on, most likely you'll be connecting your mobile device to 1/4-inch inputs.

If this is the case, you'll most likely need a stereo 1/4-inch-to-1/8-inch cable like the one shown in Figure 6.1.

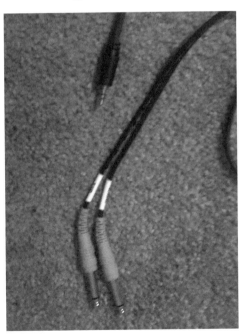

Figure 6.1   Use a 1/4-inch pair to 1/8-inch adapter to connect to your audio interface.

The purpose of the adapter in all of this is simple: The two 1/4-inch plugs on the adapter go to your audio interface, as shown in Figure 6.2.

And the 1/8-inch will go to your portable device, as shown in Figure 6.3.

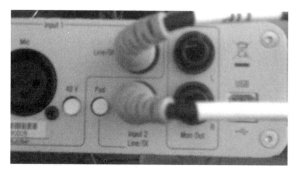

Figure 6.2   The 1/4-inch plugs go into the audio interface.

Figure 6.3   My 1/8-inch connector is going into the headphone output of my iPhone, but the headphone output on the Nintendo DS will be the same.

If you are using a first-generation iPhone (the one with the silver backing), you'll need to get another adapter due to the iPhone's recessed headphone jack. Headset Buddy makes a relatively inexpensive adapter that will fit the recessed jack and allow you to use your iPhone headphones out as a standard output. See Figure 6.4. But there are many other alternatives out there.

Just to make it easy, when connecting to your audio interface, make sure to use paired inputs, such as 1 & 2, 3 & 4, or 5 & 6. Do not use inputs that aren't commonly paired, such as 2 & 3, 4 & 5, and so on. The reason why is that when you make a stereo audio track in most DAW applications, the DAW by default will always be set for the combinations 1 & 2 and so on. If you use an uncommon pair, you will need to do additional configuration, which this chapter does not cover.

Figure 6.4   If you have a first-generation iPhone, due to its recessed jack you'll need another adapter to use its headphones out as a standard output.

For the iPhone, it's also possible to use the Apple Composite AV Cable mentioned in Chapter 4, along with some 1/4-inch-to-RCA adapters. Refer to Chapter 4 for more information.

Connecting Your Mobile Device Directly to a Computer for Recording

Most computers, Mac or PC, have built-in audio inputs—for example, my MacBook Pro's audio input, shown in Figure 6.5.

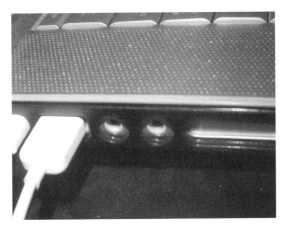

Figure 6.5   My MacBook Pro's stereo input.

While a direct connection to a computer is perfectly acceptable by the computer, it is much better to hook your mobile device to an audio interface if you have one. In most cases, audio interfaces have much better analog-to-digital converters, which helps to capture exactly what's coming from your mobile device, ensuring there isn't much generation loss.

An audio interface is even more desired when it comes to the PC platform. Audio inputs on PC laptops, as well as built-in audio inputs on desktops, are usually of cheaper quality and are not designed for music at all. Also, they tend to have severe latency in audio applications, and they can be difficult to configure. There is ASIO4ALL, www.asio4all.com, a freeware ASIO driver for all generic cards, but it can be hit or miss. And it still leaves the problem of questionable audio converters.

If you're on a Mac, your built-in port can be handy when you're in coffee shops and an interface isn't available—it isn't subject to latency issues due to Apple's Core Audio. However, a good interface is still a better recommendation.

Without sounding like I've been endorsed corporately, M-Audio does have a decent line of low-end audio interfaces, such as the M-Audio Transit USB, shown in Figure 6.6.

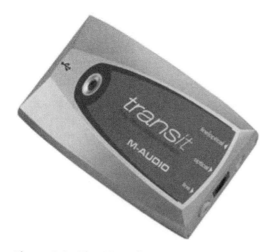

Figure 6.6   The M-Audio Transit USB.

And PreSonus offers the Inspire 1394, shown in Figure 6.7. Both go for around $79.99. Everything has to have a .99 at the end, huh?

First Recording: Tap Tempo

In many cases, getting audio to your computer will be the simplest and crudest method. Unfortunately, with devices such as the iPhone, Nintendo DS, and so on, it's usually the only option you have—connecting directly to the computer, either through interface or to your built-in audio device, with no synchronization.

Just to remind you about synchronization, it's the process of getting your handheld audio device and your computer audio playing in the same tempo.

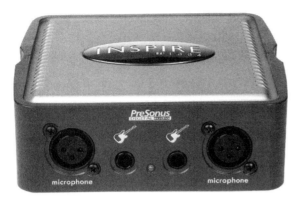

Figure 6.7 PreSonus Inspire 1394.

For example, I have a cool beat on my computer, and I have a cool melodic loop on my Nintendo DS. I would like for them to play together in perfect time. Even though I put my Nintendo DS music application at the same tempo as my computer's music application and start both applications at the same time, the audio seems to drift out of time.

As I mentioned in the introduction to this chapter, this is a simple reality. The manufacturers of handheld devices don't usually keep musicians in mind when they make the hardware. This makes it very difficult for app makers to create applications that can sync with computers because the necessary components either are not on the device or are off limits through code.

But there are many ways to get audio in sync once it's recorded in. For the moment, let's just go through a recording setup in Ableton Live. I recommend this application because it has a unique feature not common in most DAWs: tap tempo. Essentially, the way tap tempo works is simple. You tap the Tap Tempo button to the beat of what you want to record, and Ableton attempts to adjust its master tempo so that it matches yours. If you don't understand yet, don't worry—we'll go through it completely later in this section.

Even if you don't own Ableton, you can download the demo, which allows recording and saving for up to 30 days. If you decide you like it, don't feel that you have to get the full-blown Ableton Live; there are a few different versions of Live that range in price. To begin this exercise, make sure you are in the Session view of Ableton Live. If you are unsure of which is which, simply look it up in the Ableton manual.

I'll start off by connecting a 1/8-inch-stereo-to-1/8-inch stereo audio cable to the audio input of my MacBook Pro. See Figure 6.8.

Figure 6.8   Take a 1/8-inch-to-1/8-inch stereo cable and plug one end into this port on your MacBook Pro and the other to your handheld device—in this case, a Nintendo DS.

Next, I'll open up Ableton Live and go to Ableton Preferences by clicking on Live > Preferences (see Figure 6.9). If you're on a PC, go to Options > Preferences.

In the Preferences menu, click the Audio tab on the left. See Figure 6.10.

Figure 6.9   Go to Ableton Live Preferences.

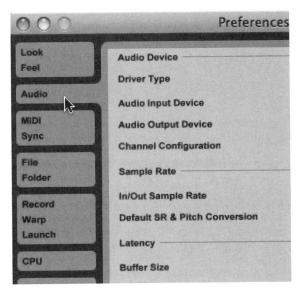

Figure 6.10   Choose the Audio tab.

In the Audio Preferences, for your audio input device choose Built-In Input, and for your audio output device choose Built-In Output (see Figure 6.11).

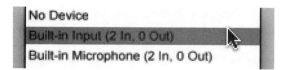

Figure 6.11   Change the audio input device to your built-in input or audio interface. Change your audio output device to your built-in output or audio interface.

If you're on a PC, simply locate your built-in input, or if you are using an audio interface, choose the appropriate inputs and outputs. However, if you're using an audio interface on a PC, make sure you select the ASIO driver. The ASIO driver will ensure better latency during recording—though latency isn't really an issue in this exercise, because we already know what we're recording will be completely out of sync.

While you are in Audio Preferences, click the Input Config button and select 1/2 (Stereo) (see Figure 6.12). This tells Ableton to record your left and right signals coming from your portable device.

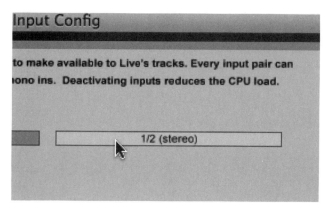

Figure 6.12   Select Input Config and make sure that 1/2 (Stereo) is highlighted.

I'll close up Preferences now, and we're ready to test our levels. I'll choose an audio track or create one by pressing Command+T. On a PC, this would be Ctrl+T. Or, you can go through the Create menu, as shown in Figure 6.13.

In your I/O section of this track, it should say Ext In. The next row below it should say 1/2. See Figure 6.14.

Press the Record Arm button, shown in Figure 6.15, and play something off of your portable device to verify that there is signal coming into Ableton Live. Your meters in Ableton should start moving (see Figure 6.15).

It's important to note that your levels should not appear as red or jump past the small gray line in Ableton. If this is the case, you will get a distorted recording coming from

Figure 6.13   Create an audio track or choose an existing one in your session.

Figure 6.14   Make sure that your inputs are Ext In and 1/2 for your I/O section.

Figure 6.15 Record arm your track and play something off your portable device to make sure you are getting signal into Ableton Live.

your portable device. To mend this, simply turn down the volume of your portable device until your meters are coming close to, but not hitting, the gray line (see Figure 6.16).

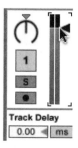

Figure 6.16 What's coming in from your portable device should not cause red meters or levels that hit the small gray line.

Press the Tab button on your typing keyboard to switch to the Arrangement view. This view of Ableton will be more familiar to Pro Tools, Cubase, and Logic Pro users. It has the familiar track lanes, as shown in Figure 6.17.

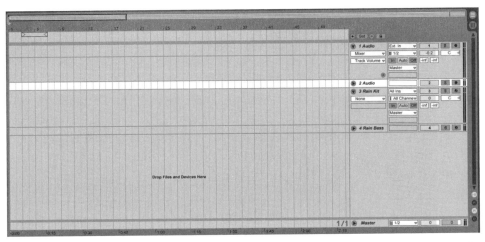

Figure 6.17 The Arrangement view is similar to other programs, such as Pro Tools and Cubase.

This next part will require a little bit of concentration to master, but once you do it a few times, it will be pretty easy. Start playing a loop or a melody from your portable device. Because we've record armed the track already, you should be able to hear it playing through just fine. If what you're recording is simply a tone with no form of rhythm, record your sound and skip to another section—this is just for rhythm and melody. For rhythm, locate the Tap Tempo button in the upper-right corner of Ableton's interface, as shown in Figure 6.18.

Figure 6.18 Locate the Tap Tempo button.

While the rhythm or melody is playing, tap along with it as if you were the metronome: 1, 2, 3, 4, 1, 2, 3, 4 . . . . As you do this, you'll notice the tempo of Ableton starting to change (see Figure 6.19). Remember to do this on a four count; don't get creative with the rhythm, or you will throw off the tempo.

Figure 6.19 As you tap tempo, you'll notice that Ableton's tempo changes.

Once you feel like you are in time and you notice the tempo in Ableton matches the tempo on your handheld device (or you're just confident), press the Metronome button in Ableton Live, as shown in Figure 6.20.

Figure 6.20   Press the Metronome button to hear whether or not you are in time.

If your tapping was done properly, the metronome will be in perfect time with your portable device melody or loop. If not, it will be out of time and somewhat annoying to listen to. If you're out of time, I recommend turning off the metronome and trying again, because having two beats going simultaneously can make it hard to get an accurate tempo. Keep trying until they are in time.

Any DAW, whether it be Cubase, Logic Pro, or Pro Tools, has a click track or metronome. This function is so important because it lets you know how fast the computer thinks the song is.

If you aren't in time with the metronome, you're out of time with the song, and this can cause severe problems later when you try to add tracks, loops, quantize parts, and so on. I mentioned this earlier in the chapter, but I want to reemphasize paying attention to the metronome when syncing loops, audio files, and so on.

When you are sure that you have both Ableton and your portable device playing in as close to perfect tempo as possible, press the Record button at the top of Ableton's interface, as shown in Figure 6.21.

Figure 6.21   Press the Record button.

At this point, you're recording your portable device in tempo with the host tempo of Ableton Live. This will make it seriously easy to put other loops, drum beats, and melodies along with what you've done on your device. Or, simply use a full song made on your handheld as a map for what you want to create in your final production.

It is important to note that if you are recording a full song from your portable device, after a while the tempo might drift slightly out of time. Thankfully, you're using Ableton. It makes it very easy to fix timing problems.

Let's learn how!

Tempo Correction

Whether you're fixing a little bit of drifting tempo (where the song or loop eventually starts to get out of time with the host application's metronome) or you're importing a loop or song where you don't know the original tempo, this section is for you!

In this section, we're going to use Ableton Live to find the actual tempo of a drum loop from a portable device (on my end, my iPhone using BeatMaker) and use Ableton's Warp Markers to make sure the drum loop is always in the right tempo no matter how many times we change Ableton's master tempo.

First, let's try it out with a regular audio loop that I recorded, which you can download at www.courseptr.com/downloads. I've placed the audio loop, testloop.aif, on my desktop, as shown in Figure 6.23. I drag this audio file into the Session view of Ableton Live, specifically in a large gray area that says Drop Files and Devices Here. See Figure 6.22.

Figure 6.22   Drag the audio file from the desktop into the gray Drop Files and Devices Here area.

Instantly, a new audio track is created, and my loop is placed within the track lane; see Figure 6.23. Pretty swanky . . . But is it in time, or no?

I press the clip's Launch button, shown in Figure 6.24. I notice that the loop is playing in a different tempo, but that's only because Live's master tempo is set at a different tempo

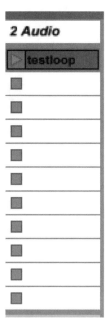

Figure 6.23   Live instantly creates a new audio track for me and places my audio loop neatly inside the track lane.

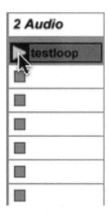

Figure 6.24   I press the clip's Launch button and then enable Ableton's metronome to see whether the loop is in time.

than this loop. I press the Metronome button to see how in tempo or out of tempo the loop is—more easily explained by saying in sync or out of sync. See Figure 6.24.

This has been a short tutorial for loops, because Ableton found the right tempo and perfectly warped the loop without any additional work needed. Live is a well-oiled machine when it comes to beat detection, and the only things that usually throw it off are things like vocals that don't necessarily have a beat, sustained notes from strings, and so on.

Ableton's ease of use for this kind of work is exactly why I recommend it for portable devices. If we would have tried this in any other DAW, it would have taken several more steps. Ableton did it in only two, those specifically being drag and drop.

Use another DAW? Don't want to use Ableton exclusively? Did you know that through a widely used protocol found in almost every DAW—Pro Tools, Cubase, and Logic Pro included—you can sync Ableton Live like a slave to your host application? For example, I can launch Pro Tools, and from within Pro Tools launch Ableton Live— and then Ableton Live is synced perfectly with Pro Tools. From there, I can record audio coming from Ableton Live into a Pro Tools track.

Let's put this in perspective for portable devices. Launch Pro Tools, launch Ableton, create a track in Pro Tools, and drag a loop into Ableton. Ableton puts the loop in perfect tempo, and I record the loop into Pro Tools. Close Ableton.

Believe it or not, this is actually quicker than trying to sync an audio file from within Pro Tools. While Pro Tools has a similar warping capability, it doesn't work as quickly as Ableton, and it requires several more steps.

If you are interested in learning more about ReWire and how you can use it to sync applications so that you can use capabilities of two or more programs at the same time, check out my other book, *Using Rewire: Skill Pack* (Course Technology PTR, 2008).

It's also possible to use Warp Markers in programs such as Ableton, Pro Tools, and Logic Pro to fix the timing of a song that drifted while you were recording it due to the tempo being slightly off.

Warp Markers, as they are called in Ableton, Pro Tools, and so on, are tiny markers that can be found in the audio editing windows of each application (though each in a different way, of course). Shown in Figure 6.25, Warp Markers allow you to simply pick up a part of an audio file and move it over without cutting into the audio, but instead stretching it.

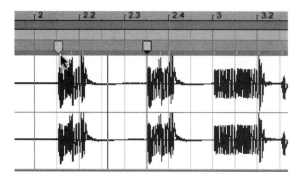

Figure 6.25 Warp Markers allow you to stretch/warp/bend your audio into the proper tempo.

By stretching particular points of audio where drifting occurs, you are able to see (through waveforms) and move drum hits and so on to the beat where they should really be occurring.

Through use of its Tempo Nudge buttons, shown in Figure 6.26, Ableton actually allows you to slow down and increase the tempo along with what you're recording, so that once you're finished, Warp Markers are already in place, taking much of the work out of tempo correction.

Figure 6.26 Nudge buttons let you correct tempo drifts while you are recording. The left button is Nudge Back, and the right button is Nudge Forward.

For example, suppose I'm recording a song in real time from my Game Boy. Initially, when I started tap tempoing, I got Ableton in perfect sync with my Game Boy, but the tempo slowly started to drift after a while. Rather than stopping the recording, I hold the Nudge Back button and listen to the Ableton metronome get closer and closer to the actual beat of my Game Boy. As soon as both Ableton and my Game Boy are in sync again, I let go of the Nudge Back button.

Or, another example: I notice the tempo in Ableton is starting to fall behind my Game Boy drum beat. This time, I press the Nudge Forward button and cause Ableton's tempo to quickly speed up so that it is once again in sync with the Game Boy.

In either example, what Ableton ends up doing when the Nudge buttons are pushed is distributing Warp Markers during the recording, basically warping audio back into beat. This beats actually cutting into the audio, which would cause loud pops to be audible in the final recording. See Figure 6.27 for a picture of an audio file that had nudges occur during the actual recording. Notice the small groups of Warp Markers in certain places throughout the audio file?

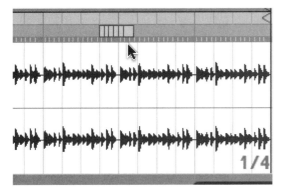

Figure 6.27   An example of a recording where Nudge buttons were used.

If you're curious to learn more about Warp Markers within Ableton Live, Pro Tools, or Logic Pro, there are in-depth illustrations on how to use them in books such as *Ableton Live 8 Power!* by Jon Margulies, *Logic Pro 9 Power!* by Kevin Anker and Orren Merton, and *Pro Tools 8 Power!* by Christopher R. Burns, Colin MacQueen, and Steve Albanese (all published by Course Technology PTR). Additionally, you can find video tutorials all over YouTube.com giving you real-time instruction on how they work.

Conclusion

This chapter illustrated some very simple methods for recording on your portable audio device. You learned about options within your DAW that make this process easy, especially for older portable devices that will never get an upgrade.

I personally have had some strong inspirations for songs after bringing in some of the "out there" beats and sounds I've created while just sitting around. Even when I didn't necessarily use what I'd created on the iPhone, my Game Boy, or even my PSP, I was able to make some wonderful loops that I used for later tracks. Because these loops were already warped in the Ableton sense, I had original custom loops later that I could just drop in on a moment's notice during sessions or live performances or for some nice spice for remixes.

In the next chapter, we'll go into some more advanced methods for tracking audio coming from your portable device. And we'll check out some of the advanced functions of some particular apps mentioned earlier in the book that make portable devices fun not only to record with, but also to perform with.

7   Studio Integration Part 2

In the previous chapter, you learned some of the basic principles of recording on a portable device. In this chapter we'll carry on with these basics, but we'll also focus on recording and integrating a device that has more advanced features, such as MIDI sync, MIDI exporting, and audio exporting.

Because there are new audio apps coming out every second, even if you don't have some of the programs or apps mentioned in this chapter, don't worry—let them give you an idea for features in future apps going forward that might be important to you. Every app maker, program developer, and nighttime code-jockey out there will always include a list of features that are available before you purchase the product. Start keeping an eye out for key features such as, "MIDI synchronization over Wi-Fi network," "Can export audio files and MIDI files," or even "Can share files over network."

Sometimes the program may seem dinky and insignificant at first, but when you see features like these appear within the 100 other things it does, you might find a hidden gem within that could really inspire and further your sound.

Also, remember that getting to know one application really well is far better than collecting a new one each week. Sometimes, through continued use, you learn new tricks within an application that you, and sometimes even the developer, never thought of.

Let's start off by looking at what is, in my opinion, one of the most valuable studio integration options out there.

MIDI Synchronization

In the previous chapter, we did exercises where we were trying to tap tempo to synchronize the host tempo with the portable device's tempo. We also did exercises where we attempted to do tempo correction after recording.

What if there was an option that allowed your DAW to send tempo information to your portable device?

MIDI synchronization is a very common option that is mostly found either within hardware or in MIDI-based music devices. Essentially, when two devices (for example, a computer and a drum machine) are connected and MIDI synchronization is enabled, both devices will start playing at the same time, and both will play in the exact same tempo. Yes, I may have mentioned this in other parts of the book, but it never hurts to have a refresher before really going into it.

As mentioned in Chapter 4, some iPhone apps (and some Nintendo apps as well) have MIDI sync capability. As mentioned earlier, BassLine by Finger-Pro has this ability. In this section, we'll take a quick peek at how it works when you set up MIDI sync over a wireless network. And if you think about it, having sync set up over a wireless network is pretty handy, because no cords whatsoever are required.

To start off, I'll need MidiBroadcast, which can be downloaded from Finger-Pro.com. Unfortunately, this application is currently only for the Mac; however, do follow the example because as this section ends, we'll be going into the DAW setup for this, and that's the same on both platforms. And the DAW setup is usually the trickiest part to learn.

So, I download MidiBroadcast and follow the installation procedure, which is the usual Mac installation of downloading and dragging to your Applications folder, as shown in Figure 7.1.

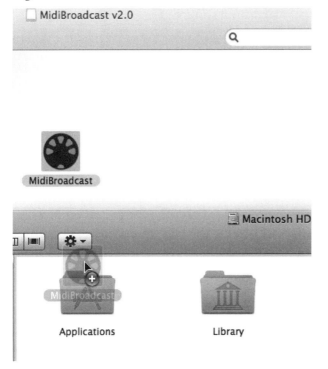

Figure 7.1 Drag MidiBroadcast into your Applications folder.

The next part involves creating a network with the AirPort built in on most Apple computers, which will be shared with an iPod Touch or an iPhone. If you need the Internet at the moment, I'd advise exploring this part later, when you don't need the Internet, because following this procedure will cut you off from it.

I'll be doing this exercise in Leopard; however, Snow Leopard won't be much different. For Tiger, you may need to do a little digging in the network settings to get this to work. Or, if you're not too handy with networking, get a knowledgeable friend to help you.

First, click on the AirPort icon in the upper-right corner of your desktop near the clock, as shown in Figure 7.2.

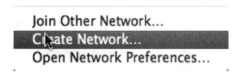

Figure 7.2   Click on the AirPort icon on your menu bar.

In the AirPort menu, choose Create Network (see Figure 7.3). A simple menu will appear. Create a name for your new network; it can be anything. For expediency of this exercise, I'd advise against setting a password.

Figure 7.3   Choose Create Network.

Now, let's run MidiBroadcast by simply double-clicking the MidiBroadcast icon in the Applications folder, as shown in Figure 7.4.

Figure 7.4   Open MidiBroadcast.

MidiBroadcast is a very simple application. As such, there's not a lot to see in it, as shown in Figure 7.5. Make sure that the Source drop-down menu says MidiBroadcast Virtual Destination. Determining what the destination is set to will require a few additional steps. We'll come back to this in a second.

Figure 7.5   The MidiBroadcast interface. Simple, eh?

Go to your Apple menu and choose System Preferences. See Figure 7.6.

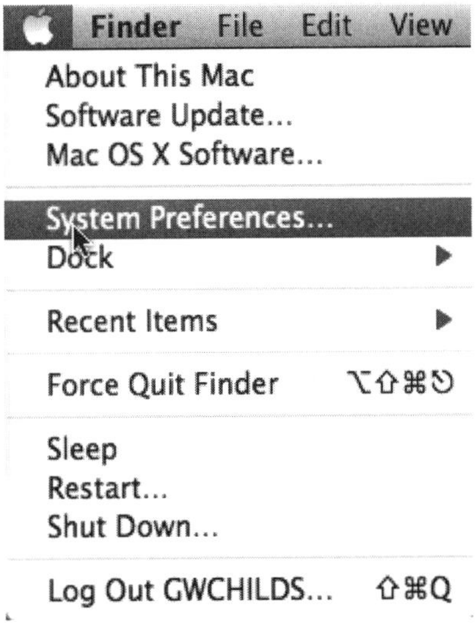

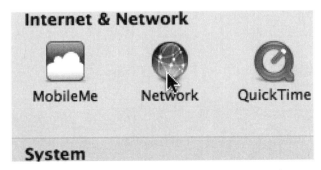

Figure 7.6   Go to your Apple menu and choose System Preferences.

In the System Preferences menu, choose Network, as shown in Figure 7.7.

Figure 7.7   In System Preferences, choose Network.

In the Network settings, click the AirPort and then click the Advanced button, as shown in Figure 7.8.

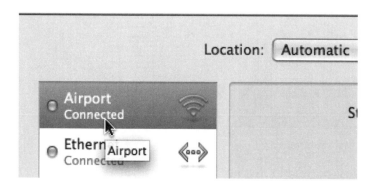

Figure 7.8   Select your AirPort and then click the Advanced button.

While in the Advanced Networking panel of your Apple System Preferences, choose the TCP/IP tab, as shown in Figure 7.9.

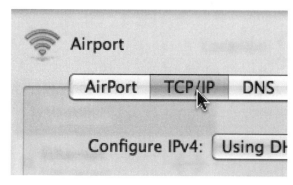

Figure 7.9   Go to the TCP/IP page.

Note the IPv4 Address in the TCP/IP page. You'll want to choose the most similar IP address that you can find in MidiBroadcast's Destination drop-down menu. In my case, my IPv4 address starts with 169.254; therefore, I will choose 169.254.255.255. The first two sets of numbers match, and that ensures that my iPhone and my laptop will communicate. See Figure 7.10.

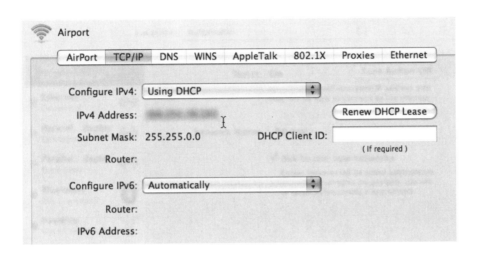

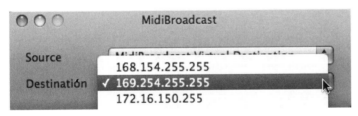

Figure 7.10   Determine your IPv4 address and then choose the closest destination in MidiBroadcast.

On your iPhone or iPod Touch, go to your Settings page and select Wi-Fi. On the Wi-Fi page, choose your network. Mine is named Ad-hoc, as shown in Figure 7.11.

Now that my iPhone is joined to my new network that I created earlier in this section, I can start up BassLine. See Figure 7.12.

In BassLine, I'll choose a current project or even one of the demos. It doesn't matter; I can always create a new one later. The important thing is that BassLine and MidiBroadcast are going before I start my DAW.

Okay, hopefully either you own or you've downloaded the Ableton demo, as instructed in the previous chapter. If not, you will need to consult your owner's manual for your own DAW on how to set up MIDI sync. Here's how you do it in Ableton Live.

Figure 7.11   Go to Settings on your iPhone or iPod Touch, choose Wi-Fi, and then select your newly created network.

Figure 7.12   Start BassLine.

Launch Ableton and go into Ableton's Preferences. For instructions on how to do this, see the previous chapter. In the Preferences page, choose MIDI Sync, as shown in Figure 7.13.

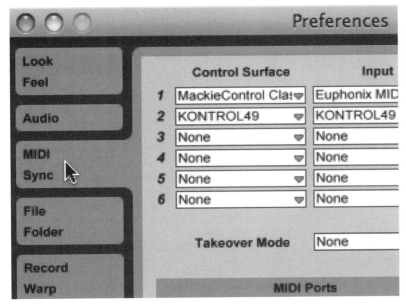

Figure 7.13   Choose the MIDI Sync page in Ableton's Preferences.

In the MIDI Sync page, there is a MIDI Ports area, shown in Figure 7.14. As you can see, I have many devices, so I'll need to scroll down to the port titled MidiBroadcast Virtual Destination. Once located, I'll press the Sync On button.

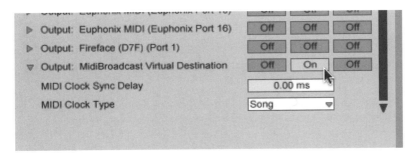

Figure 7.14   Press the Sync On button.

If you look closely, you'll notice that there is an arrow next to MidiBroadcast Virtual Destination. Pressing this arrow will give you additional options with regard to how sync will be sent to your iPhone, iPod Touch, and so on. Sync Delay lets you slightly adjust the latency in case your iPhone is off initially. MIDI Clock Type lets you adjust for triggering in Pattern mode or Song mode. For this exercise, I'll choose Pattern. See Figure 7.15.

Now for the fun part. Close up Preferences and go to the Session view. To get there, press the Tab button. Session view looks like Figure 7.16.

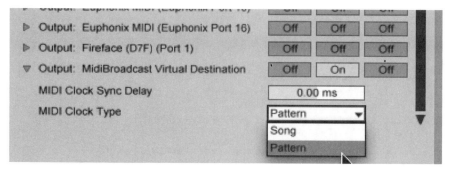

Figure 7.15   Choose Pattern mode for your MIDI Clock Type.

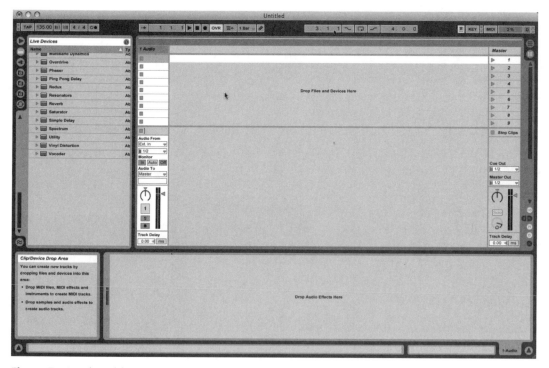

Figure 7.16   The Ableton Session view.

My iPhone is connected to the computer for this exercise. I'm going to record arm my audio track by pressing the small button that looks like a dot on Audio Track 1. See Figure 7.17. If you don't remember how to set up your portable device, please refer to the previous chapter.

Next, I'll set up my input with the channel that my iPhone is connected to. In my case, it's 7/8. See Figure 7.18.

Figure 7.17   Press the Record Arm button.

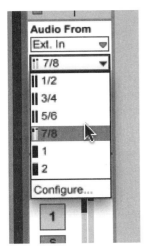

Figure 7.18   Set up your input.

Now, I'll press one of the small Record buttons within the clip lane slot, which will cause Ableton to start recording and start my iPhone to playing if I am in BassLine and everything has been done correctly up to this point. See Figure 7.19.

I have noticed that on initial launches BassLine can be a little off at first, almost as if it's trying to adjust to the tempo. If you let it run for a few seconds out of time, before you start adjusting, pressing buttons, and so on, it will generally catch up to the tempo of Ableton. Later, you can simply edit out this part of the audio. What's amazingly fun, though, is that if you turn your iPhone or iPod Touch right side up, BassLine goes into Filter mode, where you can turn the phone to the left or right, and the filter will change accordingly. You can get some really fun performances this way that will surprise you and really let you interact with the sound. See Figure 7.20.

Figure 7.19 Press a clip slot's Record button, and Ableton will start recording while the iPhone starts playing.

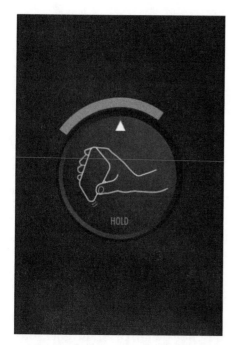

Figure 7.20 Filter mode in BassLine is really fun, and it lets you create some really cool filter performances with your wrist.

Over time, BassLine may drift out of time. Unfortunately, MIDI Sync is not always the most reliable way of working. Also, some DAWs have very reliable MIDI communications, and some don't. The most reliable MIDI transmissions I've encountered come from Logic Pro, especially for sync. However, if you get some drifting over time, just stop the Ableton sequencer by pressing the spacebar on your keyboard and then start it again.

What I really love about setting up BassLine in this way is that you're able to have this small, interactive instrument that you can rock out with almost like a guitar. You can literally get up, jump around, and create melodies that move along with drum beats and so on that you already have going in your DAW. It's very fun and very inspiring. Also, because BassLine has a very simple sequencer of its own with a lot of randomization functions, you can quickly come up with cool melodies that you would never have thought of on your own.

Audio Export

With modern DAWs, it's very easy to simply import an audio file of a drum beat, melody, and so on and then rely on the DAW to help you match the timing of what you imported. I showed you how this worked with Ableton in the previous chapter, but let me refresh your memory. I can simply drop a drum loop into Ableton, and it will automatically put the loop in time with the song I am currently working on.

Apps such as BeatMaker will also perform what's known as an *audio export* for you, which is similar to a bounce in Logic Pro and Pro Tools. Essentially, an audio export is when an audio application renders an audio file, as opposed to you having to record it in real time.

For example, suppose I have a two-bar drum beat and I set my loop locators in Beat-Maker to the beginning and end of the drum beat, as shown in Figure 7.21.

Then, I choose the Export button from the BeatMaker homepage, shown in Figure 7.22. If you're confused about how I'm navigating through BeatMaker, refer back to Chapter 5, which is all about BeatMaker.

Once I've pressed the Export button, BeatMaker will ask whether I want a MIDI export or an audio export. If you don't know what MIDI is, don't worry—it's explained more in the next section. Press the Audio button. See Figure 7.23.

What happens in the next couple of steps can be a little confusing, so please pay close attention. BeatMaker will then ask me to choose where I would like to save my audio export. You can basically choose a file path. I'll choose My Exports so that I can find it easily, and then I'll press Save. See Figure 7.24. At this point BeatMaker will prompt me to name the file. I'll choose the name Test.

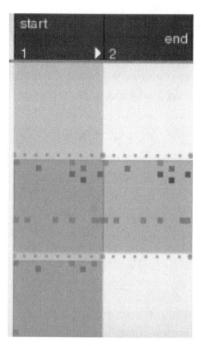

Figure 7.21   Set your loop locators in BeatMaker.

Figure 7.22   Press the Export button on the homepage in BeatMaker.

Figure 7.23   Choose Audio as the export option.

Figure 7.24   Choose a file path within BeatMaker.

Now for the confusing part (at least until I explain it): How do I get my audio file from BeatMaker? For this, I need a wireless network. Thankfully, I have one at home, like almost everybody does. I can verify that I'm connected via Wi-Fi by the Wi-Fi icon at the top of my iPhone or iPod Touch. See Figure 7.25.

Figure 7.25   Verify that you have Wi-Fi.

I start off by going to the homepage of BeatMaker again and pressing the small icon nestled at the top of the screen. I also launch BeatPack, a supplemental program (for PC and Mac) found at intua.net that allows your laptop to transfer things such as patches, audio, MIDI, and so on back and forth from your iPhone or iPod Touch. See Figure 7.26.

After downloading and installing BeatPack, I'll launch it on my laptop. As shown in Figure 7.27, it's a very simple interface with only two pages—one for kit creation and

Figure 7.26   Press the BeatPack/Intua icon on the homepage. Make sure you have your glasses on!

one named Share Kits and Samples. Realistically, BeatPack's main page is where you go to choose where you want to download files to and upload them from BeatMaker.

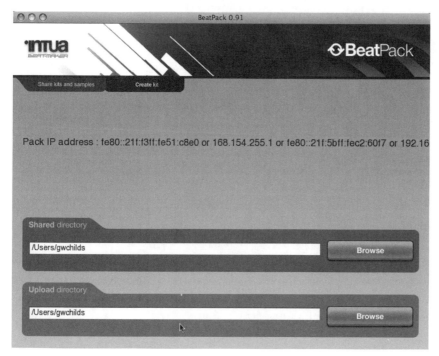

Figure 7.27   BeatPack is a very simple application for your computer that allows you to share files to and from your Apple portable device.

I've made a dedicated BeatMaker-labeled folder within my user folder. This makes it easy to keep track of things coming from and going to my iPhone (see Figure 7.28).

Figure 7.28   I've made a dedicated BeatMaker folder on my computer so that I can easily manage what comes from and goes to my iPhone.

If you look closely at BeatPack, you'll notice that it tells you the IP address of the computer that you're currently running it on. This is where BeatPack can be a little clunky. You'll notice that addresses are displayed all the way across the page, to the point that they cut off. As a result, you have to try servers through trial and error sometimes, until you get the right one.

If I look at the BeatPack page on my iPhone now, on the homepage I see two servers available at the bottom of the page, as shown in Figure 7.29.

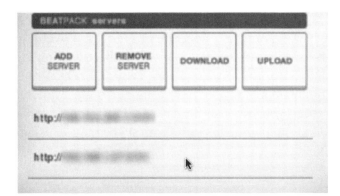

Figure 7.29   BeatMaker shows the available servers.

I choose the bottom IP address, starting with 192. Then I press the Upload button, shown in Figure 7.30. My laptop actually gave two IP options—one starting with 164 and one starting with 192. The 164 address did not work in an earlier attempt.

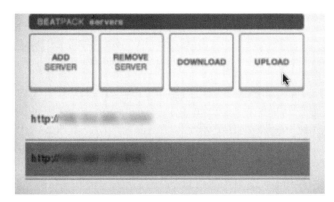

Figure 7.30   Choose a server and then press Upload.

After I press the Upload button, BeatMaker asks me to choose the file that I want to upload. I go into My Exports, where I stored my audio export earlier in this exercise, select test.wav, and then press the green Upload button. See Figure 7.31.

Figure 7.31   Navigate to the test.wav file and press the Upload button.

If the IP address is correct, the transfer should only take a second or two. It's very quick. Now I can navigate to my dedicated BeatMaker folder, and test.wav is there waiting for me. I can drag the loop/audio file directly into Ableton, Pro Tools, or another DAW and integrate it into my project or use it to create a new one. Importing audio into Ableton was explained in the previous chapter, but you will also find instructions for doing this operation in the owner's manual for Ableton or any other application you may be using. It's a standard feature across all DAWs.

MIDI Export

You may decide that you love the work you've done on your mobile device, but you don't really care for the sounds you had available. Or maybe you just know that you have much better sounds available on your computer in terms of plug-ins and so on.

For example, suppose that using a really cool application called Xewton Music Studio, I play out a nice piano melody while waiting at a bus stop. I think the melody would be a perfect beginning for a new song. But, while the Xewton piano sounds great for an iPhone application, I have a much better piano available in GarageBand. Instead of importing a recording of my piano line, like we did in the previous exercise, I'd like to import MIDI so I can edit the melody, move notes around, change note lengths, and so on.

You see, the main difference between MIDI and audio is that they are entirely different. Whereas audio is an actual recording, MIDI is computer instructions for playing back notes. I used this example earlier in the book: MIDI works similarly to a music box. A music box plays back a recorded song not through audio recordings, but through small bumps that actually force a small ping off of the tiny metal piano inside the music box (see Figure 7.32). The faster you turn the handle, the faster those small bumps cause keys to play on the small piano within.

When you record MIDI, you are actually recording those little bumps—or in this case, pulses. Each time you hit a note on your keyboard, drum pad, or iPhone, the computer records what note you played, how long you held the note, and so on. Later, when you play back a MIDI recording, the computer plays the instrument exactly the way you did previously.

Figure 7.32 In a music box, each bump causes a note to play. In MIDI, each recorded pulse causes a note to play.

What's so powerful about MIDI is that you can easily go back and move notes around, extend the lengths of the notes, change how loud the note was played, and more. And you can change the instrument at any moment that a MIDI recording is triggering, which allows you a lot of flexibility.

For example, perhaps I love the piano melody that I played, but after I play back my MIDI recording, I decide it would sound better as an organ. I press a button, and the melody is played back as an organ instead of as a piano.

Xewton Music Studio, shown in Figure 7.33, is the closest thing I've seen to Garage-Band for the iPhone...and that's not a bad thing! Although GarageBand is considered a beginner application, it is actually quite powerful because it's no-nonsense—you get in there and start laying down music rather than getting bogged down in a lot of buttons, parameters, and so on.

Like GarageBand, Xewton has tons of ready-to-go software instruments with large piano keys that you can use to easily play in melodies. When you're finished, you can go over to Xewton's extensive Tracks mode, which is really just an arrangement mode that is very, very similar to GarageBand.

Xewton Music Studio is also very handy as a portable composition tool, because its MIDI Export function makes it effortless to move your compositions from your portable device to your DAW, as you'll see in this chapter.

Figure 7.33   Xewton Music Studio—GarageBand for your pocket.

Like Xewton Music Studio, BeatMaker, the application that I used in the previous section, has a MIDI Export function. However, because BeatMaker is so sample-oriented, whatever MIDI you import from it may require some extra editing or may be completely nonsensical. There's really no way around this, though—that's just what happens with sampled audio parts. If you want to use MIDI from BeatMaker, simply follow the directions in the previous section and press the MIDI button I pointed out, instead of Audio, when doing an export.

Xewton Music Studio's instruments are essentially General MIDI instruments; therefore, any MIDI exported from Xewton will have instructions for GarageBand and others on what kind of instrument track should be set up for the MIDI part.

For example, I recorded drums and a bass synthesizer part in Xewton Music Studio. When I export MIDI from Xewton to GarageBand, GarageBand automatically sets up a bass synth and a drum track for my imported parts. And although they don't sound exactly like Xewton Music Studio's instruments, they are quite close, and they give me a reference so that I can hear what part is what and find a new sound within GarageBand that is either close or better. For example, after experimentation, I may determine that the bass part would sound better as a fretless bass.

For this section, let me give you a quick walkthrough for getting MIDI from Xewton Studio into GarageBand.

After finishing up my work in Xewton Studio, I go to the Projects panel at the top. See Figure 7.34.

Figure 7.34   Go to the Projects panel in Xewton Music Studio.

In this window, I'll press the Save button on the right, as shown in Figure 7.35. This will bring up a keyboard so that I can enter a name for my project. I'll call it Handheld.

Figure 7.35   Press the Save button and give your project a name.

Once the project has been saved, it will appear in the project list below. Outside of what's shown in Figure 7.36, there are a lot of demos that come with Xewton Music Studio. As such, I will need to scroll down the list with my finger to find my project and then tap it so that it's highlighted.

SONG	Demo - Yankee Doodle Rock	1:44
SONG	Handheld	0:06
MIDI	Kermit	0.46kB
SONG	Kermit	0:06
MIDI	Shasta	0.18kB
SONG	Shasta	0:02

Figure 7.36   Scroll down the list to locate your project and tap it so that it's highlighted.

Once I've highlighted my project, a few other buttons on the right will light up, letting me know that they are options. I press the Export button, as shown in Figure 7.37.

Figure 7.37 With my project highlighted, I press the Export button.

Similarly to BeatMaker, Xewton Music Studio asks whether I'd like to do a MIDI or an audio export. I choose MIDI this time, as shown in Figure 7.38.

Figure 7.38 Choose the MIDI option for export.

Now, if I look in my project list within the Projects panel, I'll see Handheld.mid within the list, as shown in Figure 7.39.

Now I need to get the MIDI file to the computer. I press the Server button in the lower-right corner of the screen (see Figure 7.40).

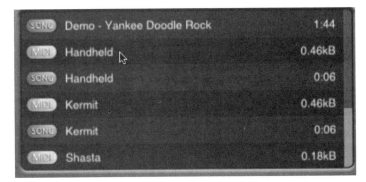

Figure 7.39   Once it's exported, I'll see Handheld.mid in my project list.

Figure 7.40   Press the Server button.

Once the Server button is pressed, Xewton Music Studio will broadcast your project files directly from your Apple device, making them available from a website only accessible over your wireless network. A screen like the one shown in Figure 7.41 will appear, telling you the website to go to in order to retrieve your files.

Figure 7.41   This window will tell you the web location of your files.

You can simply type this web address into your web browser; the download page looks like what you see in Figure 7.42.

Type	Filename	Size	Date
SONG	Demo - Amazing Grace.xms	18.9 Kb	Dec 6, 2009 11:24 AM
SONG	Demo - Blue Danube (Performance Test).xms	326.1 Kb	Dec 6, 2009 11:24 AM
SONG	Demo - Drunken Sailor Remix.xms	18.4 Kb	Dec 6, 2009 11:24 AM
SONG	Demo - Eine kleine Nachtmusik (Mozart).xms	12.4 Kb	Dec 6, 2009 11:24 AM
SONG	Demo - Formen Remix (Rosensprung).xms	30.1 Kb	Dec 6, 2009 11:24 AM
SONG	Demo - HipHop Beat.xms	34.8 Kb	Dec 6, 2009 11:24 AM
SONG	Demo - Jazzblues.xms	27.0 Kb	Dec 6, 2009 11:24 AM
SONG	Demo - Reggae.xms	19.2 Kb	Dec 6, 2009 11:24 AM
SONG	Demo - Techno.xms	19.8 Kb	Dec 6, 2009 11:24 AM
SONG	Demo - Toccata Progressive.xms	24.7 Kb	Dec 6, 2009 11:24 AM
SONG	Demo - Yankee Doodle Rock.xms	29.9 Kb	Dec 6, 2009 11:24 AM
MIDI	Handheld.mid	0.5 Kb	Feb 24, 2010 4:12 PM
SONG	Handheld.xms	1.1 Kb	Feb 24, 2010 4:11 PM
MIDI	Kermit.mid	0.5 Kb	Feb 18, 2010 6:56 PM
SONG	Kermit.xms	1.1 Kb	Feb 18, 2010 6:55 PM
MIDI	Shasta.mid	0.2 Kb	Feb 16, 2010 2:47 PM
SONG	Shasta.xms	0.4 Kb	Feb 16, 2010 2:47 PM

Select All   Select None   Invert Selection   Search   Delete Files

File Upload

Figure 7.42   The Xewton Music Studio project download page.

This download page is handy in the sense that you can access your files remotely, delete files, upload files, and more. The only thing that may be vague is how you download from it. Simply right-click on the file that you want to download and select Download Linked File As. See Figure 7.43.

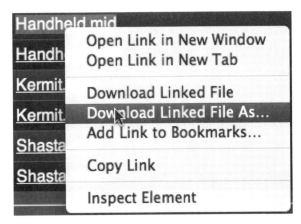

Figure 7.43   Right-click on your file and select Download Linked File As.

I've chosen to save my MIDI file on the desktop. I launch GarageBand at this point. When it comes up, I drag the MIDI file into the GarageBand arrangement window. See Figure 7.44.

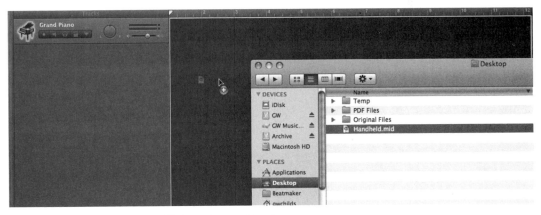

Figure 7.44   I drag my MIDI file into GarageBand.

As soon as I drop the MIDI file, GarageBand makes an instrument track for every track in my MIDI project, and it also attempts to match the instruments that I was using within Xewton Music Studio. From here, I can change sounds, try different drum sets—complete freedom.

Conclusion

If you think about it, it's not really that tough to get your music from your Apple device to the computer. It really just takes a little time to get to know some of the features that aren't usually at the top of the list. But as you can see, these features really add a whole new dimension to the workflow by allowing you to get those portably created creations into your home studio for some serious production.

Appendix: Upcoming Technology

I would hate to end things without giving you a heads up on some things to look out for that were not available when this book was written. These upcoming items could be game changers!

The iPad

As I write this, I am anxiously awaiting my iPad, which is supposed to ship in a couple of weeks. Yes, I got my preorder in!

The iPad, shown in Figure A.1, is supposed to be able to access the exact same software the iPhone and iPod Touch can. For example, you could run BeatMaker on the iPad.

One thing that gives the iPad a huge advantage is its screen size. As you can imagine, it can be kind of cumbersome tapping out beats or melodies or even doing automation on a small iPhone. On an iPad, though, it's like actually having a regular-sized drum machine right in front of you that can also access the Internet, let you read books, and more. Also, think of the iPad with applications like the iTM software listed in Chapter 4. You could control your mix using the iTM MCU (Mackie Control Unit), for example.

The only apparent limitations for this device for the use of audio production would be the single stereo output, like the other Apple devices have. I wouldn't be surprised at all, though, if we see some manufacturers coming out with adapters to compensate for this. And, as I mentioned earlier, if you're using the iPad as a controller with software like the iTM MCU, no audio is required for this type of software.

There are some very big possibilities with the iPad that I highly encourage you to think over. Or, like me, you may have preordered an iPad already!

The Akai SynthStation25

I have very high hopes for this product. The Akai SynthStation25, shown in Figure A.2, is essentially a 25-key keyboard controller that not only houses an iPhone or iPod Touch, but also interfaces with the Apple devices.

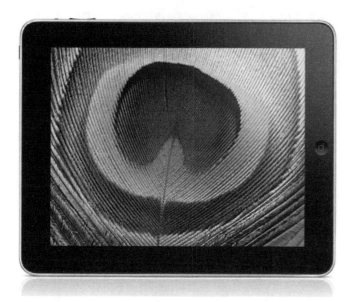

Figure A.1   The iPad could potentially be a game changer.

Figure A.2   The SynthStation25 is a controller that houses and interfaces with the iPod Touch and iPhone.

Not only will the SynthStation interact with software also provided by Akai, who have been major music manufacturers for years (Akai MPCs, samplers . . . you name it), but it will also provide RCA audio outputs and MIDI.

The software that will go on your iPod Touch or iPhone that will allow interaction with the SynthStation is completely cool as well. It gives you a portable production studio made up of synthesizers, a drum machine, a sequencer, and effects. There's even an arpeggiator.

This device and software are true game changers because they let you tap into the power of your iPhone and iPod Touch, and they give you new ways to integrate them into your home studio through MIDI and audio ports done professionally by a highly renowned company.

Nintendo DSi XL

Nintendo also has something in the works, the Nintendo DSi XL, which really only features two larger screens. While not necessarily a game changer, a bigger screen means bigger buttons for your music apps and a larger interface for music editing and more control. See Figure A.3.

Figure A.3   The Nintendo DSi XL features a larger screen.

Conclusion

So that wraps it up for now. However, you can check in with me for more updates, tips, tricks, and videos at my website, www.gwchilds.com. Thanks for reading, and see you there!

Index